Anna

Bianca

Caprice

Maria

Ines

Dee

Pabla

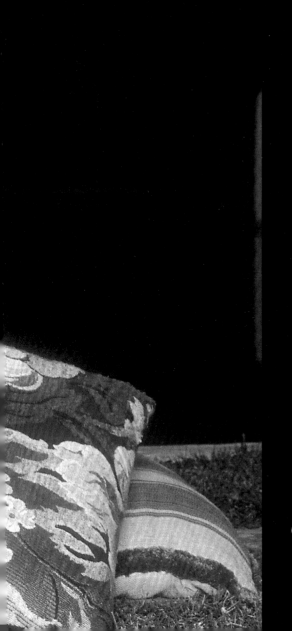

Lauren

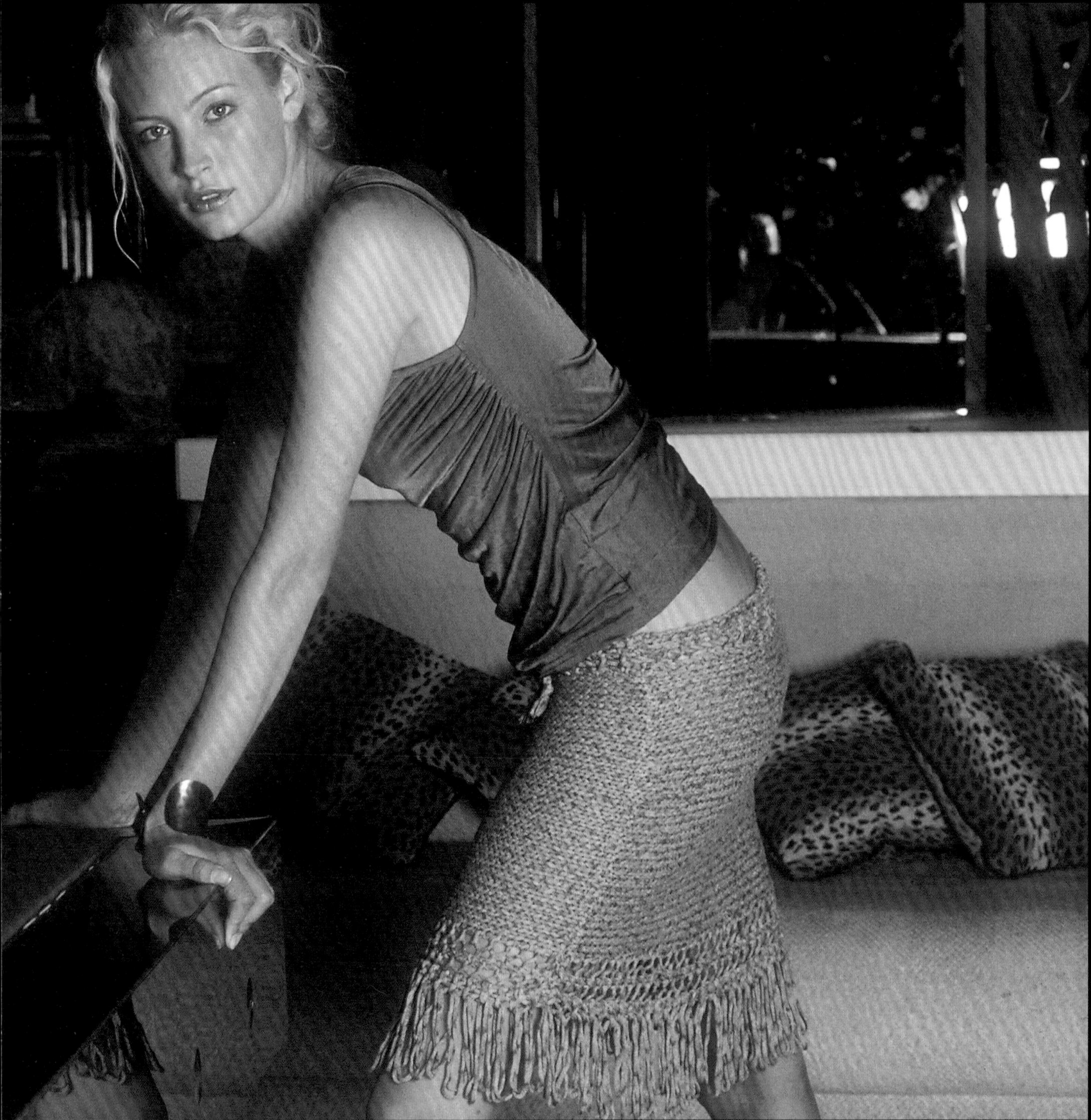

Gena

Lana

Gazella

Patrice

Andi

Luka

Sophie

LINEN PRINT

Index

Pabla

Kim Hargreaves

YARN

	XS	S	M	L	XL
To fit bust	81	86	91	97	102 cm
	32	34	36	38	40 in

Rowan Linen Print

| | 12 | 13 | 14 | 15 | 15 | x 50gm |

(photographed in Blush 342)

NEEDLES

1 pair 7mm (no 2) (US 10½) needles
1 pair 8mm (no 0) (US 11) needles

TENSION

13 sts and 16 rows to 10 cm measured over stocking stitch using 8mm (US 11) needles.

Pattern notes:

Due to the heavy nature of this yarn, it has a tendency to drop in length in wear. It is therefore advisable to measure knitted sections hanging from needles, rather than laid flat.

As row end edges of fronts form actual finished edges of garment it is important these edges are kept neat. Therefore all new balls of yarn should be joined in at side seam or armhole edges of rows.

BACK

Cast on 55 (59: 63: 67: 71) sts using 7mm (US 10½) needles.
Row 1 (RS): Purl.
Row 2: Knit.
Change to 8mm (US 11) needles.
Beg with a P row, work in rev st st for 18 rows.
Counting in from both ends of last row, place markers on 14th (15th: 16th: 17th: 18th) sts in from ends of row.
Row 21 (RS): P3, P2tog, P to within 1 st of first marker, P3tog (marked st is centre st), P to within 1 st of next marker, P3tog tbl (marked st is centre st), P to last 5 sts, P2tog tbl, P3.
Work 7 rows.
Row 29: As row 21.
43 (47: 51: 55: 59) sts.
Work 13 rows.
Row 43 (RS): P3, M1, (P to marked st, M1, P marked st, M1) twice, P to last 3 sts, M1, P1.
Work 11 rows.
Row 55: As row 43.
55 (59: 63: 67: 71) sts.
Work a further 9 (11: 11: 13: 13) rows, ending with a WS row. (Back should measure 40 (41: 41: 42: 42) cm.)
Shape armholes
Cast off 3 (4: 4: 5: 5) sts at beg of next 2 rows.
49 (51: 55: 57: 61) sts.
Dec 1 st at each end of next 3 (3: 5: 5: 7) rows, then on foll alt row.
41 (43: 43: 45: 45) sts.
Cont straight until armhole measures 20 (20: 21: 21: 22) cm, ending with a WS row.
Shape shoulders and back neck
Cast off 4 sts at beg of next 2 rows.
33 (35: 35: 37: 37) sts.
Next row (RS): Cast off 4 sts, P until there are 8 sts on right needle and turn, leaving rem sts on a holder.
Work each side of neck separately.
Cast off 4 sts at beg of next row.
Cast off rem 4 sts.
With RS facing, rejoin yarn to rem sts, cast off centre 9 (11: 11: 13: 13) sts, P to end.
Complete to match first side, reversing shapings.

LEFT FRONT

Cast on 32 (34: 36: 38: 40) sts using 7mm (US 10½) needles.

Row 1 (RS): P to last 7 sts, (slip next st purlwise with yarn at back (WS) of work, P1) 3 times, K1.
Row 2: P1, (K1, P1) 3 times, K to end.
Change to 8mm (US 11) needles.
Row 3: P to last 7 sts, (slip next st purlwise with yarn at back (WS) of work, P1) 3 times, pick up loop lying between needles and place this loop on right needle (note: this loop does NOT count as a st), sl last st knitwise.
Row 4: P tog the first st and the loop, (K1, P1) 3 times, K to end.
Last 2 rows set the sts - front opening edge slip st edging, 6 sts in slip st rib patt and rem sts in rev st st.
Cont as set for a further 16 rows.
Counting in from end of last row, place marker on 14th (15th: 16th: 17th: 18th) sts in from end of row.
Row 21 (RS): P3, P2tog, P to within 1 st of marker, P3tog (marked st is centre st), patt to end.
Work 7 rows.
Row 29: As row 21. 26 (28: 30: 32: 34) sts.
Work 7 rows.
Shape front slope
Row 37 (RS): P to last 12 sts, P2tog tbl, patt to end. 25 (27: 29: 31: 33) sts.
Working all front slope decreases as set by last row, cont as folls:
Work 5 rows.
Row 43 (RS): P3, M1, P to marked st, M1, P marked st, M1, patt to end.
28 (30: 32: 34: 36) sts.
Work 11 rows, dec 1 st at front slope edge on 6th (4th: 4th: 2nd: 2nd) and foll 0 (0: 0: 8th: 8th) row. 27 (29: 31: 32: 34) sts.
Row 55: As row 43. 30 (32: 34: 35: 37) sts.
Work a further 9 (11: 11: 13: 13) rows, dec 1 st at front slope edge of 6th (2nd: 2nd: 6th: 8th) of these rows and ending with a WS row.
29 (31: 33: 34: 36) sts.
Shape armhole
Cast off 3 (4: 4: 5: 5) sts at beg and dec 0 (1: 1: 0: 0) st at end (front slope edge) of next row.
26 (26: 28: 29: 31) sts.
Work 1 row.
Dec 1 st at armhole edge of next 3 (3: 5: 5: 7) rows, then on foll alt row **and at same time** dec 0 (0: 0: 1: 1) st at front slope edge of 0 (0: 0: next: 3rd) row. 22 sts.

Dec 1 st at front slope edge only on 2nd (4th: 2nd: 4th: 4th) and foll 12th (10th: 12th: 10th: 10th) row. 20 sts.

Cont straight until left front matches back to start of shoulder shaping, ending with a WS row.

Shape shoulder

Cast off 4 sts at beg of next and foll 2 alt rows.

Cont as set on rem 8 sts for a further 6.5 (7.5: 7.5: 8: 8) cm for back neck border extension.

Cast off.

RIGHT FRONT

Cast on 32 (34: 36: 38: 40) sts using 7mm (US 10½) needles.

Row 1 (RS): K1, (P1, slip next st purlwise with yarn at back (WS) of work) 3 times, P to end.

Row 2: K to last 7 sts, (P1, K1) 3 times, pick up loop lying between needles and place this loop on right needle (**note:** this loop does NOT count as a st), sl last st purlwise.

Change to 8mm (US 11) needles.

Row 3: K tog tbl the first st and the loop, (P1, slip next st purlwise with yarn at back (WS) of work) 3 times, P to end.

Row 4: K to last 7 sts, (P1, K1) 3 times, pick up loop lying between needles and place this loop on right needle, sl last st purlwise.

Last 2 rows set the sts - front opening edge slip st edging, 6 sts in slip st rib patt and rem sts in rev st st.

Cont as set for a further 16 rows.

Counting in from beg of last row, place marker on 14th (15th: 16th: 17th: 18th) sts in from beg of row.

Row 21 (RS): Patt to within 1 st of marker, P3tog tbl (marked st is centre st), P to last 5 sts, P2tog tbl, P3.

Work 7 rows.

Row 29: As row 21. 26 (28: 30: 32: 34) sts.

Work 7 rows.

Shape front slope

Row 37 (RS): Patt 10 sts, P2tog, P to end. 25 (27: 29: 31: 33) sts.

Working all front slope decreases as set by last row, complete to match left front, reversing shapings.

SLEEVES (both alike)

Cuff edging

Cast on 9 sts using 8mm (US 11) needles.

Row 1 (RS): K1, (P1, slip next st purlwise with yarn at back (WS) of work) 4 times.

Row 2: (P1, K1) 4 times, pick up loop lying between needles and place this loop on right needle (note: this loop does NOT count as a st), sl last st purlwise.

Row 3: K tog tbl the first st and the loop, (P1, slip next st purlwise with yarn at back (WS) of work) 3 times, P1, pick up loop lying between needles and place this loop on right needle (note: this loop does NOT count as a st), sl last st knitwise.

Row 4: P tog the first st and the loop, (K1, P1) 3 times, K1, pick up loop lying between needles and place this loop on right needle, sl last st purlwise.

Rep rows 3 and 4 until cuff edging measures 33 (33: 34.5: 36: 36) cm.

Cast off.

Main section

With RS facing and using 8mm (US 11) needles, pick up and knit 43 (43: 45: 47: 47) sts along one edge of cuff edging.

Beg with a K row, cont in rev st st as folls:

Work 1 row.

Next row (RS): P3, P2tog, P to last 5 sts, P2tog tbl, P3.

Work 3 rows.

Rep last 4 rows once more, then first of these rows (the dec row) again. 37 (37: 39: 41: 41) sts.

Work 11 rows, ending with a WS row.

Next row (RS): P3, M1, P to last 3 sts, M1, P3.

Working all increases as set by last row, inc 1 st at each end of 26th (14th: 14th: 14th: 8th) and every foll 0 (12th: 14th: 14th: 10th) row until there are 41 (43: 45: 47: 49) sts.

Cont straight until sleeve measures 43 (43: 44: 44: 44) cm **from lower edge of cuff edging**, ending with a WS row.

Shape top

Cast off 2 (3: 3: 4: 4) sts at beg of next 2 rows. 37 (37: 39: 39: 41) sts.

Dec 1 st at each end of next 3 rows, then on foll alt row, then on every foll 4th row until 25 (25: 27: 27: 29) sts rem.

Work 1 row, ending with a WS row.

Dec 1 st at each end of next and every foll alt row to 21 sts, then on foll 3 rows, ending with a WS row.

Cast off rem 15 sts.

PRESS as described on the information page. Join both shoulder seams using back stitch, or mattress stitch if preferred. Join cast-off ends of back neck border extensions, then sew one edge to back neck.

See information page for finishing instructions, setting in sleeves using the set-in method.

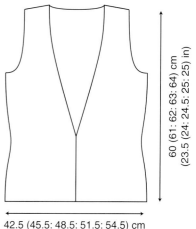

60 (61: 62: 63: 64) cm
(23.5 (24: 24.5: 25: 25) in)

42.5 (45.5: 48.5: 51.5: 54.5) cm
(16.5 (18: 19: 20.5: 21.5) in)

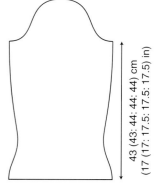

43 (43: 44: 44: 44) cm
(17 (17: 17.5: 17.5: 17.5) in)

Maria

KIM HARGREAVES

	XS	S	M	L	XL	
To fit bust	81	86	91	97	102	cm
	32	34	36	38	40	in

Rowan Linen Print

| | 10 | 10 | 11 | 12 | 12 | x 50gm |

(photographed in Refresher 344)

NEEDLES

1 pair 7mm (no 2) (US 10½) needles
1 pair 8mm (no 0) (US 11) needles

EXTRAS - 1 m of leather thonging

TENSION

13 sts and 16 rows to 10 cm measured over
stocking stitch using 8mm (US 11) needles.

Pattern note: Due to the heavy nature of this
yarn, it has a tendency to drop in length in wear.
It is therefore advisable to measure knitted sections
hanging from needles, rather than laid flat.

BACK

Cast on 55 (59: 63: 67: 71) sts using 7mm
(US 10½) needles.

Row 1 (RS): Purl.
Row 2: Purl.
Change to 8mm (US 11) needles and shape
hem as folls:
Row 1 (RS): K to last 15 sts, wrap next st (by
slipping next st on left needle to right needle,
taking yarn to opposite side of work between
needles and then slipping same st back onto left
needle - on foll row work the wrapped st and
the loop tog as one st) and turn.
Row 2: P to last 15 sts, wrap next st and turn.
Row 3: K to last 11 sts, wrap next st and turn.
Row 4: P to last 11 sts, wrap next st and turn.
Row 5: K to last 8 sts, wrap next st and turn.
Row 6: P to last 8 sts, wrap next st and turn.
Row 7: K to last 5 sts, wrap next st and turn.
Row 8: P to last 5 sts, wrap next st and turn.
Row 9: K to last 2 sts, wrap next st and turn.
Row 10: P to last 2 sts, wrap next st and turn.
Row 11: Knit to end.
Beg with a P row, work in st st across all sts for
5 rows, ending with a WS row.
Next row (dec) (RS): K2, K2tog, K to last 4 sts,
K2tog tbl, K2.
Working all decreases as set by last row, dec 1 st
at each end of 4th and foll 4th row, then on foll
alt row. 47 (51: 55: 59: 63) sts.
Work 7 rows, ending with a WS row.
Next row (inc) (RS): K2, M1, K to last 2 sts,
M1, K2.★★
Working all increases as set by last row, inc 1 st
at each end of every foll 6th row until there are
55 (59: 63: 67: 71) sts.
Work a further 5 (7: 7: 9: 9) rows, ending with a
WS row. (Back measures approx 37 (38: 38: 39:
39) cm at centre.)
Shape armholes
Cast off 2 (3: 3: 4: 4) sts at beg of next 2 rows.
51 (53: 57: 59: 63) sts.
Dec 1 st at each end of next 3 (3: 5: 5: 7) rows,
then on foll 2 alt rows.
41 (43: 43: 45: 45) sts.
Cont straight until armhole measures 20 (20: 21:
21: 22) cm, ending with a WS row.
Shape shoulders and back neck
Cast off 4 sts at beg of next 4 rows.
Next row (RS): Cast off 4 sts, P to last 4 sts,
K to end.
Next row: Cast off 4 sts, P to end.
Cast off rem 17 (19: 19: 21: 21) sts.

FRONT

Work as given for back to ★★, ending with a RS
row.
Working all side seam increases as set by last row,
cont as folls:
Work 3 rows, ending with a WS row.
Divide for front opening
Next row (RS): K23 (25: 27: 29: 31), pick up
loop lying between needles and place this loop
on right needle (note: this loop does NOT
count as a st), slip next st knitwise and turn,
leaving rem sts on a holder. 24 (26: 28: 30: 32) sts.
Work each side of neck separately.
Next row: P tog the first st and the loop, P to
end.
Last 2 rows set slip st edging along front
opening edge.
Next row (eyelet row) (inc) (RS): K2, M1,
K to last 4 sts, yfwd, K2tog tbl (to form eyelet),
patt 2 sts. 25 (27: 29: 31: 33) sts.
Last row sets position of eyelets.
Making a further 4 eyelets on every foll 10th
row and noting that no further reference will be
made to eyelets, cont as folls:
Work 3 rows, ending with a WS row.
Next row (dec) (RS): K to last 4 sts, K2tog tbl,
patt 2 sts. 24 (26: 28: 30: 32) sts.
Working all front opening edge decreases as set
by last row, cont as folls:
Work 1 row, ending with a WS row.
Inc 1 st at side seam edge of next and foll 6th
row **and at same time** dec 1 st at front
opening edge of 7th row. 25 (27: 29: 31: 33) sts.
Work a further 5 (7: 7: 9: 9) rows, ending with a
WS row. (Front should match back to beg of
armhole shaping.)
Shape armhole
Cast off 2 (3: 3: 4: 4) sts at beg and dec 0 (0: 0: 1:
1) st at end of next row. 23 (24: 26: 26: 28) sts.
Work 1 row.
Dec 1 st at armhole edge of next 3 (3: 5: 5: 7)
rows, then on foll 2 alt rows **and at same time**
dec 1 st at front opening edge of 3rd (next: next:
5th: 5th) and foll 0 (6th: 6th: 0: 6th) row.
17 (17: 17: 18: 17) sts.
Dec 1 st at front opening edge **only** on
2nd (6th: 6th: 2nd: 4th) and every foll 6th (4th:
4th: 4th: 4th) row to 15 (12: 12: 12: 12) sts,
then on every foll 4th (-: -: -: -) row until 12 (-:
-: -: -) sts rem.

Cont straight until front matches back to start of shoulder shaping, ending with a WS row.

Shape shoulder

Cast off 4 sts at beg of next and foll alt row.

Work 1 row.

Cast off rem 4 sts.

With RS facing, rejoin yarn to rem sts, and cont as folls:

Next row (RS): K2tog, K to end.

24 (26: 28: 30: 32) sts.

Work each side of neck separately.

Next row: P to last st, pick up loop lying between needles and place this loop on right needle (**note**: this loop does NOT count as a st), sl last st purlwise.

Next row (eyelet row) (inc) (RS): K tog tbl first st and the loop, K1, K2tog, yfwd (to form eyelet), K to last 2 sts, M1, K2.

25 (27: 29: 31: 33) sts.

Last 2 rows set slip st edging along front opening edge and position of eyelets.

Making a further 4 eyelets on every foll 10th row, cont as folls:

Work 3 rows, ending with a WS row.

Next row (dec) (RS): Patt 2 sts, K2tog, K to end. 24 (26: 28: 30: 32) sts.

Working all front opening edge decreases as set by last row, complete to match first side, reversing shapings.

LEFT SLEEVE

Back section

Cast on 10 (10: 11: 12: 12) sts using 7mm (US 10½) needles.

**Row 1 (RS): Purl.

Row 2: Purl.

Row 3: P to last st, take yarn to back of work, pick up loop lying between needles and place this loop on right needle (**note**: this loop does NOT count as a st), sl last st knitwise.

Row 4: P tog first st and the loop, P to end.

Change to 8mm (US 11) needles.

Row 5: K to last st, pick up loop lying between needles and place this loop on right needle, sl last st knitwise.

Row 6: As row 4.

Last 2 rows set slip st edging with rem sts in st st. Cont as set for a further 10 rows, ending with a WS row.

Next row (inc) (RS): K2, M1, patt to end.

Break yarn and leave sts on a holder.**

Front section

Cast on 23 (23: 24: 25: 25) sts using 7mm (US 10½) needles.

***Row 1 (RS): Purl.

Row 2: P to last st, pick up loop lying between needles and place this loop on right needle (**note**: this loop does NOT count as a st), sl last st purlwise.

Row 3: K tog tbl the first st and the loop, P to end.

Row 4: As row 2.

Change to 8mm (US 11) needles.

Row 5: K tog tbl the first st and the loop, K to end.

Row 6: As row 2.

Last 2 rows set slip st edging with rem sts in st st. Cont as set for a further 10 rows, ending with a WS row.

Next row (inc) (RS): Patt to last 2 sts, M1, K2.***

Join sections

With **WS** facing, P across 24 (24: 25: 26: 26) sts of front section, then P across 11 (11: 12: 13: 13) sts of back section. 35 (35: 37: 39: 39) sts.

****Beg with a K row and working all increases as set, cont in st st, shaping sides by inc 1 st at each end of 11th (7th: 9th: 9th: 7th) and every foll 14th (10th: 10th: 10th: 8th) row to 39 (43: 45: 47: 49) sts, then on every foll 12th (-: -: -: -) row until there are 41 (-: -: -: -) sts.

Cont straight until sleeve measures 43 (43: 44: 44: 44) cm, ending with a WS row.

Shape top

Cast off 2 (3: 3: 4: 4) sts at beg of next 2 rows. 37 (37: 39: 39: 41) sts.

Dec 1 st at each end of next 3 rows, then on foll alt row, then on every foll 4th row until 25 (25: 27: 27: 29) sts rem.

Work 1 row, ending with a WS row.

Dec 1 st at each end of next and every foll alt row to 21 sts, then on foll 3 rows, ending with a WS row. Cast off rem 15 sts.

RIGHT SLEEVE

Front section

Cast on 23 (23: 24: 25: 25) sts using 7mm (US 10½) needles.

Work as given for back section of left sleeve from ** to **.

Back section

Cast on 10 (10: 11: 12: 12) sts using 7mm (US 10½) needles.

Work as given for front section of left sleeve from *** to ***.

Join sections

With **WS** facing, P across 11 (11: 12: 13: 13) sts of back section, then P across 24 (24: 25: 26: 26) sts of front section. 35 (35: 37: 39: 39) sts.

Complete as given for left sleeve from ****.

MAKING UP

PRESS as described on the information page.

Join both shoulder seams using back stitch, or mattress stitch if preferred.

See information page for finishing instructions, setting in sleeves using the set-in method.

Thread thonging in and out of eyelets as in photograph.

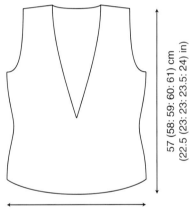

57 (58: 59: 60: 61) cm
(22.5 (23: 23: 23.5: 24) in)

42.5 (45.5: 48.5: 51.5: 54.5) cm
(16.5 (18: 19: 20.5: 21.5) in)

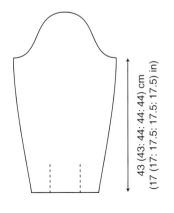

43 (43: 44: 44: 44) cm
(17 (17: 17.5: 17.5: 17.5) in)

GABRIELLA

KIM HARGREAVES

YARN

	XS-M	M-XL	
To fit bust	81-91	91-102	cm
	32-36	36-40	in

Rowan Linen Print

	16	19	x	50gm

(photographed in Moody 348)

NEEDLES

1 pair 7mm (no 2) (US 10½) needles
1 pair 8mm (no 0) (US 11) needles

TENSION

13 sts and 16 rows to 10 cm measured over stocking stitch using 8mm (US 11) needles.

Pattern note: Due to the heavy nature of this yarn, it has a tendency to drop in length in wear. It is therefore advisable to measure knitted sections hanging from needles, rather than laid flat.

BACK

Cast on 73 (85) sts using 7mm (US 10½) needles.
Beg with a P row, work in rev st st for 3 rows, ending with a RS row.

Change to 8mm (US 11) needles and cont in patt as folls:
Row 1 (WS): Purl.
Row 2: (K2tog tbl, K4, yfwd) 0 (1) time, ★K1, yfwd, K4, slip next 2 sts tog as though to K2tog, K1, pass 2 slipped sts over, K4, yfwd, rep from ★ to last 1 (7) sts, K1, (yfwd, K4, K2tog) 0 (1) time.
These 2 rows form patt.
Cont in patt until back measures 58 cm, ending with a WS row.
Shape armholes
Keeping patt correct, cast off 4 (5) sts at beg of next 2 rows. 65 (75) sts.
Dec 1 st at each end of next 3 (5) rows, then on foll 3 (4) alt rows. 53 (57) sts.
Cont straight until armhole measures 23 (25) cm, ending with a WS row.
Shape shoulders and back neck
Cast off 5 (6) sts at beg of next 2 rows. 43 (45) sts.
Next row (RS): Cast off 5 (6) sts, patt until there are 10 (9) sts on right needle and turn, leaving rem sts on a holder.
Work each side of neck separately.
Cast off 4 sts at beg of next row.
Cast off rem 6 (5) sts.
With RS facing, rejoin yarn to rem sts, cast off centre 13 (15) sts, patt to end.
Complete to match first side, reversing shapings.

LEFT FRONT

Cast on 37 (43) sts using 7mm (US 10½) needles.
Beg with a P row, work in rev st st for 3 rows, ending with a RS row.
Change to 8mm (US 11) needles and cont in patt as folls:
Row 1 (WS): Purl.
Row 2: (K2tog tbl, K4, yfwd) 0 (1) time, ★K1, yfwd, K4, slip next 2 sts tog as though to K2tog, K1, pass 2 slipped sts over, K4, yfwd, rep from ★ to last st, K1.
These 2 rows form patt.
Cont in patt until left front matches back to beg of armhole shaping, ending with a WS row.
Shape armholes
Keeping patt correct, cast off 4 (5) sts at beg of next row. 33 (38) sts.
Work 1 row.

Dec 1 st at armhole edge of next 3 (5) rows, then on foll 3 (4) alt rows.
27 (29) sts.
Cont straight until 13 (15) rows less have been worked than on back to start of shoulder shaping, ending with a RS row.
Shape neck
Keeping patt correct, cast off 5 sts at beg of next row. 22 (24) sts.
Dec 1 st at neck edge of next 4 rows, then on foll 2 (3) alt rows. 16 (17) sts.
Work 4 rows, ending with a WS row.
Shape shoulder
Cast off 5 (6) sts at beg of next and foll alt row.
Work 1 row.
Cast off rem 6 (5) sts.

RIGHT FRONT

Cast on 37 (43) sts using 7mm (US 10½) needles.
Beg with a P row, work in rev st st for 3 rows, ending with a RS row.
Change to 8mm (US 11) needles and cont in patt as folls:
Row 1 (WS): Purl.
Row 2: ★K1, yfwd, K4, slip next 2 sts tog as though to K2tog, K1, pass 2 slipped sts over, K4, yfwd, rep from ★ to last 1 (7) sts, K1, (yfwd, K4, K2tog) 0 (1) time.
These 2 rows form patt.
Complete to match left front, reversing shapings.

SLEEVES (both alike)

Cast on 37 (39) sts using 7mm (US 10½) needles.
Beg with a P row, work in rev st st for 3 rows, ending with a RS row.
Change to 8mm (US 11) needles and cont in patt as folls:
Row 1 (WS): Purl.
Row 2: K0 (1), ★K1, yfwd, K4, slip next 2 sts tog as though to K2tog, K1, pass 2 slipped sts over, K4, yfwd, rep from ★ to last 1 (2) sts, K1 (2).
These 2 rows form patt.
Cont in patt, shaping sides by inc 1 st at each end of 16th and every foll 14th (12th) row to 43 sts, then on every foll 12th (10th) row until there are 45 (49) sts, taking inc sts into st st.
Cont straight until sleeve measures 42 (43) cm, ending with a WS row.

Shape top

Keeping patt correct, cast off 4 (5) sts at beg of next 2 rows. 37 (39) sts.

Dec 1 st at each end of next 3 rows, then on foll alt row, then on every foll 4th row until 23 (25) sts rem.

Work 1 row, ending with a WS row.

Dec 1 st at each end of next and foll 0 (1) alt row, then on foll 3 rows, ending with a WS row. Cast off rem 15 sts.

MAKING UP

PRESS as described on the information page. Join both shoulder seams using back stitch, or mattress stitch if preferred.

Front band

Cast on 10 sts using 7mm (US 10½) needles.

Row 1 (RS): K1, ★P1, slip next st purlwise with yarn at back (WS) of work, rep from ★ 3 times more, K1.

Row 2: K1, (P1, K1) 4 times, pick up loop lying between needles and place this loop on right needle (**note**: this loop does NOT count

as a st), slip last st purlwise.

Row 3: K tog tbl first st and the loop, ★P1, slip next st purlwise with yarn at back (WS) of work, rep from ★ 3 times more, K1.

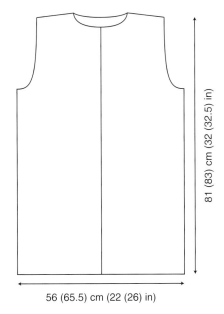

81 (83) cm (32 (32.5) in)

56 (65.5) cm (22 (26) in)

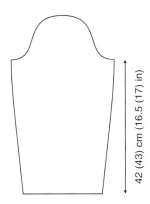

42 (43) cm (16.5 (17) in)

Rep last 2 rows until band, when slightly stretched, fits up right front opening edge, around entire neck edge and down left front opening edge, ending with a WS row. Cast off. Slip stitch band in place, ensuring the slip st edging side of the band is left free.

See information page for finishing instructions, setting in sleeves using the set-in method.

Design number 4

Rae

KIM HARGREAVES

YARN

Rowan Linen Print

A Blush	342	4	x	50gm
B Crush	347	1	x	50gm

(also photographed in A - Moody 348 and B - Pip 346)

NEEDLES

1 pair 8mm (no 0) (US 11) needles
1 pair 10mm (no 000) (US 15) needles

TENSION

11 sts and 16 rows to 10 cm measured over pattern using 10mm (US 15) needles.

FINISHED SIZE

Completed scarf is approx 15 cm (6 in) wide and 180 cm (71 in) long, excluding fringe.

SCARF

Cast on 16 sts using 10mm (US 15) needles and yarn A.

Row 1 (RS): K1, ★yfwd, P2tog, rep from ★ to last st, K1.

Row 2: As row 1.

These 2 rows form patt.

Cont in patt until scarf measures 180 cm. Cast off.

MAKING UP

PRESS as described on the information page.

Fringe (make 2)

Cast on 8 sts using 8mm (US 11) needles and one strand of yarn A held together with one strand of yarn B.

Row 1 (RS): K1, yfwd, K2tog, K5.

Row 2: P4, K2, yfwd, K2tog.

Rep these 2 rows until fringe strip, unstretched, fits neatly across end of scarf, ending with a WS row.

Next row (RS): Cast off 4 sts, fasten off st on right needle, let 4 sts on left needle fall from needle and unravel down to cast-on edge to form fringe.

Slip stitch fringe in place.

See information page for finishing instructions.

Andi

KIM HARGREAVES

	XS	S	M	L	XL	
To fit bust	81	86	91	97	102	cm
	32	34	36	38	40	in

Rowan Linen Print

| | 10 | 10 | 10 | 11 | 12 | x 50gm |

(photographed in Pip 346)

NEEDLES

1 pair 8mm (no 0) (US 11) needles

TENSION

13 sts and 18 rows to 10 cm measured over lower pattern, 11 sts and 16 rows to 10 cm measured over upper pattern using 8mm (US 11) needles.

Pattern notes:

Due to the heavy nature of this yarn, it has a tendency to drop in length in wear. It is therefore advisable to measure knitted sections hanging from needles, rather than laid flat.

As row end edges of fronts form actual finished edges of garment it is important these edges are kept neat. Therefore all new balls of yarn should be joined in at side seam or armhole edges of rows.

BACK

Cast on 60 (60: 64: 68: 72) sts using 8mm (US 11) needles.

Work in lower patt as folls:

Row 1 (RS): Knit.

Row 2: P2, ★yrn, P4tog, rep from ★ to last 2 sts, P2.

Row 3: K2, ★K1, (K1, P1, K1) into yrn of previous row, rep from ★ to last 2 sts, K2.

Row 4: Knit.

Row 5: As row 2.

Row 6: As row 3.

These 6 rows form lower patt.

Cont in lower patt, dec 1 st at each end of 3rd and every foll 4th row until 50 (50: 54: 58: 62) sts rem. (**note:** as number of sts varies whilst working patt, do NOT count sts after patt row 2 or 5.)

Work 2 rows, ending with patt row 3 and a RS row.

Next row (WS): K4 (3: 2: 4: 2), K2tog, ★K3 (5: 6: 4: 5), K2tog, rep from ★ to last 4 (3: 2: 4: 2) sts, K to end. 41 (43: 47: 49: 53) sts.

Cont in upper patt as folls:

Row 1 (RS): Purl.

Row 2: K1, ★yfwd, K2tog, rep from ★ to end.

Row 3: Purl.

Row 4: ★Sl 1, K1, psso, yfwd, rep from ★ to last st, K1.

These 4 rows form upper patt.

Cont in upper patt, shaping side seams by inc 1 st at each end of 3rd and every foll 6th row until there are 49 (51: 55: 57: 61) sts, taking inc sts into patt.

Work 7 (9: 9: 11: 11) rows, ending with a WS row. (Back measures approx 36 (37: 37: 38: 38) cm.)

Shape armholes

Keeping patt correct, cast off 3 sts at beg of next 2 rows. 43 (45: 49: 51: 55) sts.

Dec 1 st at each end of next 3 rows, then on foll 0 (1: 2: 3: 4) alt rows. 37 (37: 39: 39: 41) sts.

Cont straight until armhole measures 19 (19: 20: 20: 21) cm, ending with a WS row.

Shape shoulders and back neck

Cast off 3 (3: 4: 3: 4) sts at beg of next 2 rows. 31 (31: 31: 33: 33) sts.

Next row (RS): Cast off 3 (3: 4: 3: 4) sts, patt until there are 8 (8: 7: 8: 7) sts on right needle and turn, leaving rem sts on a holder.

Work each side of neck separately.

Cast off 4 sts at beg of next row.

Cast off rem 4 (4: 3: 4: 3) sts.

With RS facing, rejoin yarn to rem sts, cast off centre 9 (9: 9: 11: 11) sts, patt to end.

Complete to match first side, reversing shapings.

LEFT FRONT

Cast on 32 (32: 36: 36: 36) sts using 8mm (US 11) needles.

Work in lower patt as folls:

Row 1 (RS): Knit.

Row 2: P2, ★yrn, P4tog, rep from ★ to last 2 sts, P2.

Row 3: K2, ★K1, (K1, P1, K1) into yrn of previous row, rep from ★ to last 2 sts, K1, pick up loop lying between needles and place this loop on right needle (**note:** this loop does NOT count as a st), slip last st knitwise.

Row 4: P tog first st and the loop, K to end.

Row 5: P2, ★yrn, P4tog, rep from ★ to last 2 sts, P1, take yarn to WS of work, pick up loop lying between needles and place this loop on right needle, slip last st knitwise.

Row 6: P tog first st and the loop, K1, ★K1, (K1, P1, K1) into yrn of previous row, rep from ★ to last 2 sts, K2.

These 6 rows form lower patt, with last 4 rows setting slip st edging.

Cont in lower patt with slip st edging, dec 1 st at beg of 3rd and every foll 4th row until 27 (27: 31: 31: 31) sts rem. (**note:** as number of sts varies whilst working patt, do NOT count sts after patt row 2 or 5.)

Work 2 rows, ending with patt row 3 and a RS row.

Next row (WS): P tog first st and the loop, K2 (2: 2: 1: 2), K2tog, ★K2 (3: 2: 3: 6), K2tog, rep from ★ to last 2 sts, K2. 21 (22: 24: 25: 27) sts.

Keeping slip st edging correct, cont in upper patt as folls:

Row 1 (RS): P to last st, patt last st.

Row 2: Patt first st, K0 (1: 1: 0: 0), ★yfwd, K2tog, rep from ★ to end.

Row 3: As row 1.

Row 4: Patt first st, K1 (0: 0: 1: 1), ★sl 1, K1, psso, yfwd, rep from ★ to last st, K1.

These 4 rows form upper patt with slip st edging.

Cont as set, shaping side seam by inc 1 st at beg of 3rd and every foll 6th row until there are 25 (26: 28: 29: 31) sts, taking inc sts into patt.

Work 1 (3: 3: 5: 5) rows, ending with a WS row.

Shape front slope

Next row (RS): Patt to last 3 sts, K2tog, patt last st. 24 (25: 27: 28: 30) sts.

Working all front slope decreases as set by last row, cont as folls:

Dec 1 st at front slope edge of 2nd (2nd: 4th: 2nd: 2nd) and foll 0 (0: 0: alt: 0) row. 23 (24: 26: 26: 29) sts.

Work 3 (3: 1: 1: 3) rows, ending with a WS row.

Shape armhole

Keeping patt correct, cast off 3 sts at beg and dec 1 (1: 0: 0: 1) st at end of next row. 19 (20: 23: 23: 25) sts.

Work 1 row.

Dec 1 st at armhole edge of next 3 rows, then on foll 0 (1: 2: 3: 4) alt rows **and at same time** dec 1 st at front slope edge of 3rd (3rd: next: next: 3rd) and every foll 0 (0: 4th: 4th: 4th) row. 15 (15: 16: 14: 15) sts.

Dec 1 st at front slope edge **only** on 4th (2nd: 2nd: 4th: 4th) and every foll 4th row until 10 (10: 11: 10: 11) sts rem.

Cont straight until left front matches back to start of shoulder shaping, ending with a WS row.

Shape shoulder

Cast off 3 (3: 4: 3: 4) sts at beg of next and foll alt row.

Work 1 row.

Cast off rem 4 (4: 3: 4: 3) sts.

RIGHT FRONT

Cast on 32 (32: 36: 36: 36) sts using 8mm (US 11) needles.

Work in lower patt as folls:

Row 1 (RS): Knit.

Row 2: P2, ★yrn, P4tog, rep from ★ to last 2 sts, P1, pick up loop lying between needles and place this loop on right needle (note: this loop does NOT count as a st), slip last st purlwise.

Row 3: K tog tbl first st and the loop, K1, ★K1, (K1, P1, K1) into yrn of previous row, rep from ★ to last 2 sts, K2.

Row 4: K to last st, bring yarn forward to WS of work, pick up loop lying between needles and place this loop on right needle, slip last st purlwise.

Row 5: K tog tbl first st and the loop, P1, ★yrn, P4tog, rep from ★ to last 2 sts, P2.

Row 6: K2, ★K1, (K1, P1, K1) into yrn of previous row, rep from ★ to last 2 sts, K1, bring yarn forward to WS of work, pick up loop lying between needles and place this loop on right needle, slip last st purlwise.

These 6 rows form lower patt, with last 4 rows setting slip st edging.

Cont in lower patt with slip st edging, dec 1 st at end of 3rd and every foll 4th row until 27 (27: 31: 31: 31) sts rem. (**Note**: as number of sts varies whilst working patt, do NOT count sts after patt row 2 or 5.)

Work 2 rows, ending with patt row 3 and a RS row.

Next row (WS): K2, K2tog, ★K2 (3: 2: 3: 6), K2tog, rep from ★ to last 3 (3: 3: 2: 3) sts, K2 (2: 2: 1: 2), patt last st. 21 (22: 24: 25: 27) sts.

Keeping slip st edging correct, cont in upper patt as folls:

Row 1 (RS): Patt first st, P to end.

Row 2: K1, ★yfwd, K2tog, rep from ★ to last 2 (1: 1: 2: 2) sts, K1 (0: 0: 1: 1), patt last st.

Row 3: As row 1.

Row 4: ★Sl 1, K1, psso, yfwd, rep from ★ to last 1 (2: 2: 1: 1) sts, K0 (1: 1: 0: 0), patt last st.

These 4 rows form upper patt with slip st edging.

Cont as set, shaping side seam by inc 1 st at end of 3rd and every foll 6th row until there are 25 (26: 28: 29: 31) sts, taking inc sts into patt.

Work 1 (3: 3: 5: 5) rows, ending with a WS row.

Shape front slope

Next row (RS): Patt first st, K2tog tbl, patt to end. 24 (25: 27: 28: 30) sts.

Working all front slope decreases as set by last row, complete to match left front, reversing shapings.

SLEEVES (both alike)

Cast on 32 (32: 36: 36: 36) sts using 8mm (US 11) needles.

Work in lower patt as given for back, shaping sides by inc 1 st at each end of 15th and foll 10th row. 36 (36: 40: 40: 40) sts.

Work a further 2 rows, ending with patt row 3 and a RS row.

Next row (WS): K5 (5: 3: 3: 6), K2tog, ★K10 (10: 6: 6: 11), K2tog, rep from ★ to last 5 (5: 3: 3: 6) sts, K to end. 33 (33: 35: 35: 37) sts.

Cont in upper patt as given for back, shaping sides by inc 1 st at each end of 15th and foll 14th row, taking inc sts into patt. 37 (37: 39: 39: 41) sts.

Cont straight until sleeve measures 42 (42: 43: 43: 43) cm, ending with a WS row.

Shape top

Keeping patt correct, cast off 3 sts at beg of next 2 rows. 31 (31: 33: 33: 35) sts.

Dec 1 st at each end of next 3 rows, then on foll alt row, then on every foll 4th row until 19 (19: 21: 21: 23) sts rem.

Work 1 row, ending with a WS row.

Dec 1 st at each end of next and every foll alt row until 15 sts rem, then on foll 3 rows, ending with a WS row. Cast off rem 9 sts.

MAKING UP

PRESS as described on the information page. Join both shoulder seams using back stitch, or mattress stitch if preferred.

Back neck edging

With RS facing and using 8mm (US 11) needles, pick up and knit 17 (17: 17: 19: 19) sts across back neck. Cast off knitwise (on WS).

See information page for finishing instructions, setting in sleeves using the set-in method. Make two twisted cords, each 45 cm long, and knot one end. Attach other end to front opening edge level with first row worked in upper patt.

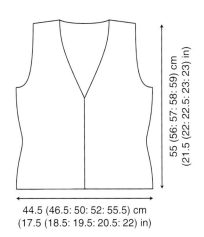

44.5 (46.5: 50: 52: 55.5) cm
(17.5 (18.5: 19.5: 20.5: 22) in)

55 (56: 57: 58: 59) cm
(21.5 (22: 22.5: 23: 23) in)

42 (42: 43: 43: 43) cm
(16.5 (16.5: 17: 17: 17) in)

Gazella

KIM HARGREAVES

YARN

	XS	S	M	L	XL	
To fit bust	81	86	91	97	102	cm
	32	34	36	38	40	in

Rowan Linen Print

| | 10 | 11 | 11 | 12 | 13 | x 50gm |

(photographed in Moody 348)

NEEDLES

1 pair 7mm (no 2) (US 10½) needles
1 pair 8mm (no 0) (US 11) needles

TENSION

13 sts and 16 rows to 10 cm measured over
stocking stitch using 8mm (US 11) needles.

Pattern note: Due to the heavy nature of this
yarn, it has a tendency to drop in length in wear.
It is therefore advisable to measure knitted sections
hanging from needles, rather than laid flat.

BACK

Cast on 58 (62: 66: 70: 74) sts using 7mm
(US 10½) needles.
Row 1 (RS): Purl.
Row 2: Knit.

Row 3: P1, ★yrn, P2tog, rep from ★ to last st, P1.
Row 4: Knit.
Change to 8mm (US 11) needles.
Beg with a P row, work in rev st st until back
measures 16 (17: 17: 18: 18) cm, ending with a
WS row.
Next row (dec) (RS): P2, P2tog, P to last 4 sts,
P2tog tbl, P2.
Working all decreases as set by last row, dec 1 st
at each end of every foll 4th row until 46 (50:
54: 58: 62) sts rem.
Work 9 rows, ending with a WS row.
Next row (inc) (RS): P2, M1P, P to last 2 sts,
M1P, P2.
Working all increases as set by last row, inc 1 st
at each end of every foll 8th row until there are
52 (56: 60: 64: 68) sts.
Cont straight until back measures 51 (52: 52: 53:
53) cm, ending with a WS row.★★
Next row (RS): K8 (10: 12: 11: 13), P to end.
Next row: P8 (10: 12: 11: 13), K to last 9 (11:
13: 12: 14) sts, P to end.
Shape armholes
Next row (RS): Cast off 8 (10: 12: 11: 13) sts,
K until there are 2 sts on right needle, P to last
9 (11: 13: 12: 14) sts, K to end.
Next row: Cast off 8 (10: 12: 11: 13) sts, P until
there are 3 sts on right needle, K to last 3 sts, P2,
pick up loop lying between needles and place
this loop on right needle (**note:** this loop does
NOT count as a st), slip last st purlwise.
36 (36: 36: 42: 42) sts.
Next row: K tog tbl first st and the loop, K1,
K3tog tbl, P to last 5 sts, K3tog, K1, pick up
loop lying between needles and place this loop
on right needle (**note:** this loop does NOT
count as a st), slip last st knitwise.
Next row: P tog first st and the loop, P2, K to
last 3 sts, P2, pick up loop lying between needles
and place this loop on right needle, slip last st
purlwise.
Last 2 rows set slip st and st st edging and
decreases.
Keeping sts and decreases correct as set, cont as folls:
Dec 2 sts at each end of next and every foll alt
row until 16 (16: 16: 18: 18) sts rem, then on foll
4th row. 12 (12: 12: 14: 14) sts.
Work 7 (7: 9: 7: 9) rows, ending with a WS row.
Next row (RS): Patt 3 sts, M1, P to last 3 sts,
M1, patt to end.

Work 1 row.
Rep last 2 rows twice more. 18 (18: 18: 20: 20) sts.
Next row (RS): Patt 3 sts, M1, **knit** to last 3 sts,
M1, patt to end.
Next row: Patt 3 sts, M1P, **knit** to last 3 sts,
M1P, patt to end. 22 (22: 22: 24: 24) sts.
Shape back neck
Next row (RS): Patt 2 sts, M1, K2 and turn,
leaving rem sts on a holder.
Work each side of neck separately.
Next row: P2tog, P1, M1P, patt 2 sts. 5 sts.
Next row: Patt 2 sts, M1, K1, K2tog.
Next row: P4, patt last st.
Cast off rem 5 sts.
With RS facing, rejoin yarn to rem sts, cast off
centre 14 (14: 14: 16: 16) sts, K to last 2 sts, M1,
patt 2 sts. 5 sts.
Complete to match first side, reversing shapings.

FRONT

Work as given for back to ★★, ending with a WS
row.
Place marker between centre 2 sts of last row.
Next row (RS): K4 (6: 8: 9: 11), P to within
3 sts of marker, K6 (marker is between centre
2 sts of this group of 6 sts), P to end.
Next row: P4 (6: 8: 9: 11), K to within 3 sts of
marker, P6 (marker is between centre 2 sts of
this group of 6 sts), K to last 5 (7: 9: 10: 12) sts,
P to end.
Divide for neck and shape armholes
Next row (RS): Cast off 2 (4: 6: 7: 9) sts, K
until there are 3 sts on right needle, P to within
4 sts of marker, K2tog, K1, pick up loop lying
between needles and place this loop on right
needle, slip next st knitwise and turn, leaving
rem sts on a holder. 23 (23: 23: 24: 24) sts.
Work each side of neck separately.
Next row: P tog first st and the loop, P2, K to
last 3 sts, P2, pick up loop lying between needles
and place this loop on right needle, slip last st
purlwise.
Next row: K tog tbl first st and the loop, K1,
K3tog tbl, P to last 5 sts, K3tog, K1, pick up
loop lying between needles and place this loop
on right needle, slip last st knitwise.
Next row: P tog first st and the loop, P2, K to
last 3 sts, P2, pick up loop lying between needles
and place this loop on right needle, slip last st
purlwise.

Last 2 rows set slip st and st st edging and decreases.

Keeping sts and decreases correct as set, cont as folls:

Dec 2 sts at neck edge of next and 1 (1: 1: 2: 2) foll 4th rows, then 1 st on 2 (2: 2: 1: 1) foll 4th row **and at same time** dec 2 sts at armhole edge of next and foll alt row, then on foll 4th row, then 1 st on foll 4th row. 6 sts.

Dec 1 st at armhole edge only on 2nd row. 5 sts.

Work 15 (15: 17: 17: 19) rows straight.

Cast off rem 5 sts.

With RS facing, rejoin yarn to rem sts, K2, K2tog tbl, P to last 5 (7: 9: 10: 12) sts, K to end.

Now working slip st and st st edging at both ends of rows, cast off 2 (4: 6: 7: 9) sts at beg of next row and complete to match first side, reversing shapings.

MAKING UP

PRESS as described on the information page.

Back neck edging

With RS facing and using 7mm (US 10½) needles, pick up and knit 20 (20: 20: 22: 22) sts across back neck edge.

Cast off knitwise (on WS).

Join both shoulder seams using back stitch, or mattress stitch if preferred. Join left side seam.

Hem fringe

Cast on 7 sts using 8mm (US 11) needles and yarn **DOUBLE**.

Row 1 (RS): K1, yfwd, K2tog, K4.

Row 2: P3, K2, yfwd, K2tog.

Rep these 2 rows until fringe strip, unstretched, fits neatly along entire cast-on edge of back and front, ending with a WS row.

Next row (RS): Cast off 3 sts, fasten off st on right needle, let 3 sts on left needle fall from needle and unravel down to cast-on edge to form fringe.

Slip stitch hem fringe in place.

Join right side seam.

See information page for finishing instructions.

73 (74: 76: 77: 78) cm (28.5 (29: 30: 30.5: 30.5) in)

40 (43: 46: 49: 52.5) cm (15.5 (17: 18: 19.5: 20.5) in)

DESIGN NUMBER 7

LAUREN

KIM HARGREAVES

YARN
Rowan Linen Print
7 x 50gm
(photographed in Refresher 344)

NEEDLES
1 pair 15mm (US 19) needles

TENSION
8 sts and 10 rows to 10 cm measured over pattern using 15mm (US 19) needles.

FINISHED SIZE
Completed shawl is approx 51 cm (20 in) wide and 160 cm (63 in) long.

SHAWL

Cast on 96 sts using 15mm (US 19) needles.

Row 1 (RS): Knit.

Row 2: P2, ★yrn, P4tog, rep from ★ to last 2 sts, P2.

Row 3: K2, ★K1, (K1, P1, K1) into yrn of previous row, rep from ★ to last 2 sts, K2.

Row 4: Cast on 4 sts, K to end.

100 sts.

Rep rows 2 to 4, 7 times more.

128 sts.

Row 26: P2, ★yrn, P4tog, rep from ★ to last 2 sts, P2.

Row 27: K2, ★K1, (K1, P1, K1) into yrn of previous row, rep from ★ to last 2 sts, K2.

Row 28: Cast off 4 sts, K to end.

124 sts.

Rep rows 26 to 28, 7 times more. 96 sts.

Rep rows 2 and 3 once more.

Cast off **loosely** knitwise (on WS).

MAKING UP

PRESS as described on the information page.

LUKA

KIM HARGREAVES

YARN

	ladies			men		
	S	M	L	M	L	XL
To fit bust/	86	91	97	102	107	112 cm
chest	34	36	38	40	42	44 in

Rowan Linen Print
V neck sweater

| A Moody 348 | 9 | 9 | 10 | 11 | 12 | 12 x 50gm |
| B Pip 346 | 8 | 9 | 9 | 10 | 11 | 11 x 50gm |

Laced neck sweater

| | 16 | 17 | 19 | 20 | 22 | 23 x 50gm |

Oddment of same yarn in contrast colour for neck lacing
(photographed in Sandy 343 with Pip 346)

NEEDLES

1 pair 7mm (no 2) (US 10½) needles
1 pair 8mm (no 0) (US 11) needles

TENSION

13 sts and 16 rows to 10 cm measured over stocking stitch using 8mm (US 11) needles.

Pattern notes:
Due to the heavy nature of this yarn, it has a tendency to drop in length in wear. It is therefore advisable to measure knitted sections hanging from needles, rather than laid flat.

The pattern is written for the 3 ladies sizes, followed by the mens sizes in **bold**. Where only one figure appears this applies to all sizes in that group.

V neck sweater

BACK
Cast on 65 (69: 73: **77: 81: 85**) sts using 7mm (US 10½) needles and yarn A.
Row 1 (RS): Purl.
Row 2: Purl.
Change to 8mm (US 11) needles.
Starting and ending rows as indicated and repeating the 12 row patt repeat throughout, cont in patt from chart as folls:
Cont straight until back measures 41 (**43**) cm, ending with a WS row.
Shape armholes
Keeping patt correct, cast off 3 (**4**) sts at beg of next 2 rows. 59 (63: 67: **69: 73: 77**) sts.
Dec 1 st at each end of next 3 rows, then on foll 1 (2: 3: **3: 4: 5**) alt rows.
51 (53: 55: **57: 59: 61**) sts.
Cont straight until armhole measures 21 (22: 23: **24: 25: 26**) cm, ending with a WS row.
Shape shoulders and back neck
Cast off 5 (**5: 5: 6**) sts at beg of next 2 rows.
41 (43: 45: **47: 49: 49**) sts.
Next row (RS): Cast off 5 (**5: 5: 6**) sts, patt until there are 9 (**9: 10: 9**) sts on right needle and turn, leaving rem sts on a holder.
Work each side of neck separately.
Cast off 4 sts at beg of next row.
Cast off rem 5 (**5: 6: 5**) sts.
With RS facing, rejoin appropriate yarn to rem sts, cast off centre 13 (15: 17: **19**) sts, patt to end.
Complete to match first side, reversing shapings.

FRONT
Work as given for back until 14 (**16**) rows less have been worked than on back to start of shoulder shaping, ending with a WS row.
Divide for neck
Next row (RS): Patt 25 (26: 27: **28: 29: 30**) sts and turn, leaving rem sts on a holder.
Work each side of neck separately.
Dec 1 st at neck edge of next 10 (11: 12: **13**) rows.
15 (**15: 16: 17**) sts.

Work 3 (2: 1: **2**) rows, ending with a WS row.
Shape shoulder
Cast off 5 (**5: 5: 6**) sts at beg of next and foll alt row.
Work 1 row. Cast off rem 5 (**5: 6: 5**) sts.
With RS facing, rejoin appropriate yarn to rem sts, K2tog, K to end.
Complete to match first side, reversing shapings.

SLEEVES (both alike)
Cast on 33 (33: 35: **37: 37: 39**) sts using 7mm (US 10½) needles and yarn A.
Row 1 (RS): Purl.
Row 2: Purl.
Change to 8mm (US 11) needles.
Starting and ending rows as indicated and repeating the 12 row patt repeat throughout, cont in patt from chart, shaping sides by inc 1 st at each end of 17th and every foll 12th (10th: 10th: **12th: 10th: 10th**) row to 39 (43: 47: **43: 47: 51**) sts, then on every foll 10th (8th: –: **10th: 8th: 8th**) row until there are 43 (45: –: **49: 51: 53**) sts, taking inc sts into patt.
Cont straight until sleeve measures 44 (46: 48: **50: 51: 52**) cm, ending with a WS row.
Shape top
Keeping patt correct, cast off 3 (**4**) sts at beg of next 2 rows. 37 (39: 41: **41: 43: 45**) sts.
Dec 1 st at each end of next 3 rows, then on foll alt row, then on every foll 4th row until 23 (25: 27: **27: 29: 31**) sts rem.
Work 1 row, ending with a WS row.
Dec 1 st at each end of next and every foll alt row to 19 sts, then on foll row, ending with a WS row. Cast off rem 17 sts.

MAKING UP
PRESS as described on the information page.
Join right shoulder seam using back stitch, or mattress stitch if preferred.
Neckband
With RS facing, using 7mm (US 10½) needles and yarn A, pick up and knit 18 (**20**) sts down left side of neck, place marker on needle, pick up and knit 18 (**20**) sts up right side of neck, then 21 (23: 25: **27**) sts from back.
57 (59: 61: **67**) sts.
Row 1 (WS): K to within 2 sts of marker, K2tog, slip marker to right needle, K2tog tbl, K to end.

Row 2: K to within 2 sts of marker, K2tog tbl, slip marker to right needle, K2tog, K to end.
Cast off knitwise (on WS).
See information page for finishing instructions, setting in sleeves using the set-in method.

Laced neck sweater

BACK

Using same colour throughout, work as for back of V neck sweater.

FRONT

Work as given for back until 10 (8: 8: **8: 8: 6**) rows less have been worked than on back to beg of armhole shaping, ending with a WS row.

Divide for neck

Next row (RS): Patt 31 (33: 35: **37: 39: 41**) sts, pick up loop lying between needles and place this loop on right needle (**note:** this loop does NOT count as a st), slip next st knitwise and turn, leaving rem sts on a holder.
32 (34: 36: **38: 40: 42**) sts.
Work each side of neck separately.

Next row: P tog first st and the loop, patt to end.
Last 2 rows set slip st edging along front opening edge.
Keeping slip st edging correct, cont as folls:

Next row (RS): Patt to last 4 sts, yrn, work 2 tog (to make eyelet), patt 2 sts.
Last row forms eyelet.
Making a further 4 eyelets in every foll 6th row and noting that no further reference will be made to eyelets, cont as folls:
Cont straight until front matches back to beg of armhole shaping, ending with a WS row.

Shape armhole

Keeping patt correct, cast off 3 (**4**) sts at beg of next row. 29 (31: 33: **34: 36: 38**) sts.
Work 1 row.
Dec 1 st at armhole edge of next 3 rows, then on foll 1 (2: 3: **3: 4: 5**) alt rows.
25 (26: 27: **28: 29: 30**) sts.
Cont straight until 14 (**16**) rows less have been worked than on back to start of shoulder shaping, ending with a WS row.

Shape neck

Dec 1 st at neck edge of next 10 (11: 12: **13**) rows.
15 (**15: 16: 17**) sts.
Work 4 (3: 2: **3**) rows, ending with a WS row.

Shape shoulder

Cast off 5 (**5: 5: 6**) sts at beg of next and foll alt row.
Work 1 row.
Cast off rem 5 (**5: 6: 5**) sts.
With RS facing, rejoin yarn to rem sts, work 2 tog, patt to end.
32 (34: 36: **38: 40: 42**) sts.

Next row (WS): Patt to last st, pick up loop lying between needles and place this loop on right needle (**note:** this loop does NOT count as a st), slip last st purlwise.

Next row: K tog tbl first st and the loop, patt 1 st, work 2 tog, yrn (to make eyelet), patt to end.
Last 2 rows set slip st edging along front opening edge, and set position of eyelets.
Complete to match first side, reversing shapings.

SLEEVES (both alike)

Using same colour throughout, work as for sleeves of V neck sweater.

MAKING UP

PRESS as described on the information page.
Join both shoulder seams using back stitch, or mattress stitch if preferred.

Neckband

With RS facing, using 7mm (US 10½) needles, starting and ending at front opening edges, pick up and knit 18 (**20**) sts up right side of neck, 21 (23: 25: **27**) sts from back, then 18 (**20**) sts down left side of neck. 57 (59: 61: **67**) sts.

Row 1 (WS): K2tog tbl, K to last 2 sts, K2tog.
Row 2: K2tog tbl, K to last 2 sts, K2tog.
Cast off knitwise (on WS).
See information page for finishing instructions, setting in sleeves using the set-in method.
Using contrast colour, make a twisted cord approx 110 cm long and thread through eyelet holes along front opening edges.

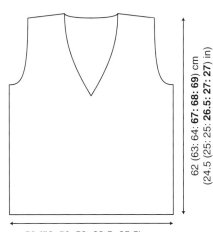

62 (63: 64: **67: 68: 69**) cm
(24.5 (25: 25: **26.5: 27: 27**) in)

50 (53: 56: **59: 62.5: 65.5**) cm
(19.5 (21: 22: **23: 24.5: 26**) in)

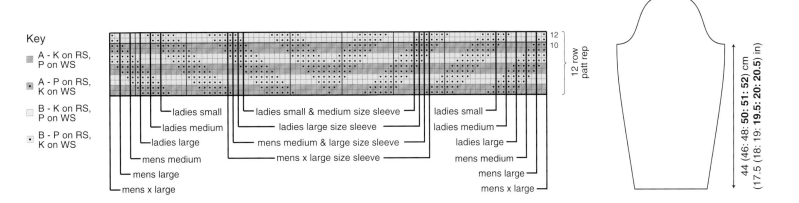

Key

- ▨ A - K on RS, P on WS
- ▣ A - P on RS, K on WS
- □ B - K on RS, P on WS
- ▨ B - P on RS, K on WS

12
10

12 row patt rep

ladies small
ladies medium
ladies large
mens medium
mens large
mens x large

ladies small & medium size sleeve
ladies large size sleeve
mens medium & large size sleeve
mens x large size sleeve

ladies small
ladies medium
ladies large
mens medium
mens large
mens x large

44 (46: 48: **50: 51: 52**) cm
(17.5 (18: 19: **19.5: 20: 20.5**) in)

Gena

KIM HARGREAVES

	XS	S	M	L	XL
To fit bust	81	86	91	97	102 cm
	32	34	36	38	40 in

Rowan Linen Print

| | 18 | 19 | 20 | 21 | 22 x 50gm |

(photographed in Pip 346)

NEEDLES

1 pair 7mm (no 2) (US 10½) needles
1 pair 8mm (no 0) (US 11) needles

TENSION

13 sts and 16 rows to 10 cm measured over
stocking stitch using 8mm (US 11) needles.

Pattern notes:

Due to the heavy nature of this yarn, it has a
tendency to drop in length in wear. It is
therefore advisable to measure knitted sections
hanging from needles, rather than laid flat.

As row end edges of fronts form actual finished
edges of garment it is important these edges are
kept neat. Therefore all new balls of yarn should
be joined in at side seam or armhole edges of rows.

BACK

Cast on 61 (65: 69: 73: 77) sts using 7mm
(US 10½) needles.
Starting and ending rows as indicated and
repeating the 12 row patt repeat throughout,
cont in patt from chart as folls:
Work 2 rows, ending with a WS row.
Change to 8mm (US 11) needles.
Cont in patt until back measures 41 (42: 42: 43:
43) cm, ending with a WS row.
Shape armholes
Keeping patt correct, cast off 6 sts at beg of next
2 rows. 49 (53: 57: 61: 65) sts.
Cont straight until armhole measures 25 (25: 26:
26: 27) cm, ending with a WS row.
Shape shoulders and back neck
Cast off 5 (6: 6: 7: 7) sts at beg of next 4 rows,
then 6 (5: 7: 6: 8) sts at beg of foll 2 rows.
Cast off rem 17 (19: 19: 21: 21) sts.

LEFT FRONT

Cast on 31 (33: 35: 37: 39) sts using 7mm
(US 10½) needles.
Starting and ending rows as indicated and
repeating the 12 row patt repeat throughout,
cont in patt from chart as folls:
Row 1 (RS): Work first 28 (30: 32: 34: 36) sts
as row 1 of chart, K3.
Row 2: P3, work last 28 (30: 32: 34: 36) sts as
row 2 of chart.
Change to 8mm (US 11) needles.
Row 3: Work first 28 (30: 32: 34: 36) sts as row
3 of chart, K2, pick up loop lying between needles
and place this loop on right needle (**note**: this
loop does NOT count as a st), sl last st knitwise.
Row 4: P tog the first st and the loop, P2, work
last 28 (30: 32: 34: 36) sts as row 4 of chart.
Last 2 rows set the sts – front opening edge slip
st and st st edging, and rem sts in patt foll chart.
Cont as set until 8 rows less have been worked
than on back to beg of armhole shaping, ending
with a WS row.
Shape front slope
Next row (RS): Patt to last 4 sts, K2tog tbl,
patt 2 sts. 30 (32: 34: 36: 38) sts.
Working all front slope decreases as set by last
row, cont as folls:
Work 7 rows, dec 1 st at front slope edge of 4th
of these rows and ending with a WS row.
29 (31: 33: 35: 37) sts.

Shape armhole
Keeping patt correct, cast off 6 sts at beg and
dec 1 st at end (front slope edge) of next row.
22 (24: 26: 28: 30) sts.
Dec 1 st at front slope edge only on 4th and every
foll 4th row to 20 (19: 22: 21: 24) sts, then on
every foll 6th row until 16 (17: 19: 20: 22) sts rem.
Cont straight until left front matches back to
start of shoulder shaping, ending with a WS row.
Shape shoulder
Cast off 5 (6: 6: 7: 7) sts at beg of next and foll
alt row.
Work 1 row.
Cast off rem 6 (5: 7: 6: 8) sts.

RIGHT FRONT

Cast on 31 (33: 35: 37: 39) sts using 7mm
(US 10½) needles.
Starting and ending rows as indicated and
repeating the 12 row patt repeat throughout,
cont in patt from chart as folls:
Row 1 (RS): K3, work last 28 (30: 32: 34: 36)
sts as row 1 of chart.
Row 2: Work first 28 (30: 32: 34: 36) sts as row
2 of chart, P2, pick up loop lying between
needles and place this loop on right needle
(**note**: this loop does NOT count as a st), sl last
st purlwise.
Change to 8mm (US 11) needles.
Row 3: K tog tbl first st and the loop, K2, work
last 28 (30: 32: 34: 36) sts as row 3 of chart.
Row 4: Work first 28 (30: 32: 34: 36) sts as row
4 of chart, P2, pick up loop lying between needles
and place this loop on right needle, sl
last st purlwise.
Last 2 rows set the sts – front opening edge slip
st and st st edging, and rem sts in patt foll chart.
Cont as set until 8 rows less have been worked
than on back to beg of armhole shaping, ending
with a WS row.
Shape front slope
Next row (RS): Patt 2 sts, K2tog, patt to end.
30 (32: 34: 36: 38) sts.
Working all front slope decreases as set by last
row, complete to match left front, reversing
shapings.

SLEEVES (both alike)

Cast on 65 (65: 67: 67: 69) sts using 7mm
(US 10½) needles.

Starting and ending rows as indicated and
repeating the 12 row patt repeat throughout,
cont in patt from chart as folls:
Work 2 rows, ending with a WS row.
Change to 8mm (US 11) needles.
Cont in patt until sleeve measures 47 (47: 48: 48:
48) cm, ending with a WS row. Cast off.

MAKING UP

PRESS as described on the information page.
Back neck edging
With RS facing and using 7mm (US 10½)
needles, pick up and knit 17 (19: 19: 21: 21) sts
across back neck.
Cast off knitwise (on WS).
Join both shoulder seams using back stitch, or
mattress stitch if preferred.
Cuff fringe (make 2)
Cast on 7 sts using 8mm (US 11) needles and
yarn **DOUBLE**.
Row 1 (RS): K1, yfwd, K2tog, K4.
Row 2: P3, K2, yfwd, K2tog.
Rep these 2 rows until fringe strip fits neatly
along cast-on edge of sleeve, ending with a WS
row.
Next row (RS): Cast off 3 sts, fasten off st on
right needle, let 3 sts on left needle fall from
needle and unravel down to cast-on edge to
form fringe.
Slip stitch cuff fringe in place.
Join side seams.
Hem fringe
Work as given for cuff fringe, making one strip
that fits neatly along entire front and back cast-
on edge.
Slip stitch hem fringe in place.
See information page for finishing instructions,
setting in sleeves using the square set-in method.

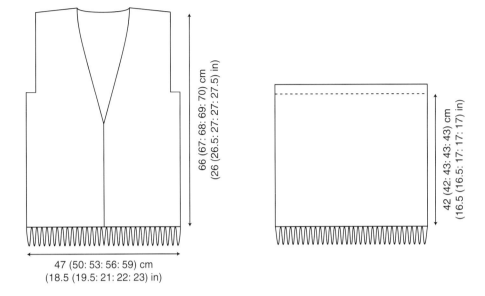

66 (67: 68: 69: 70) cm
(26 (26.5: 27: 27: 27.5) in)

47 (50: 53: 56: 59) cm
(18.5 (19.5: 21: 22: 23) in)

42 (42: 43: 43: 43) cm
(16.5 (16.5: 17: 17: 17) in)

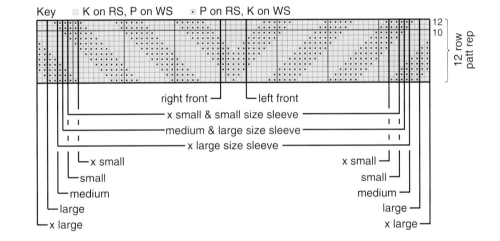

Key   ☐ K on RS, P on WS   ▨ P on RS, K on WS

12
10

12 row
patt rep

right front — — left front
— x small & small size sleeve —
— medium & large size sleeve —
— x large size sleeve —

x small   x small
small   small
medium   medium
large   large
x large   x large

L A N A

KIM HARGREAVES

YARN

	XS	S	M	L	XL
To fit hips	86	91	97	102	107 cm
	34	36	38	40	42 in

Rowan Linen Print

| | 6 | 6 | 7 | 7 | 8 x 50gm |

(photographed in Pip 346)

NEEDLES

1 pair 8mm (no 0) (US 11) needles

TENSION

13 sts and 16 rows to 10 cm measured over stocking stitch using 8mm (US 11) needles.

BACK and FRONT
(both alike, knitted sideways)

Cast on 49 (50: 51: 52: 53) sts using 8mm (US 11) needles.

Row 1 (RS): (K1, yfwd, K2tog) twice, K to last 9 sts, yfwd, K2tog, K1, yfwd, join in second ball of yarn and using yarn DOUBLE, K2tog, K4.

Row 2: Using yarn DOUBLE, P3, K2, let second ball of yarn drop and cont using original ball of yarn only as folls: yfwd, K2tog, K1, yfwd, K2tog, P21 (22: 23: 24: 25), wrap next st (by

slipping next st onto right needle, taking yarn to back (RS) of work between needles and slipping same st back onto left needle - on foll rows work the loop and wrapped st tog as one st) and turn.

Row 3: K to last 9 sts, yfwd, K2tog, K1, yfwd, using yarn DOUBLE, K2tog, K4.

Row 4: Using yarn DOUBLE, P3, K2, let second ball of yarn drop and cont as folls: yfwd, K2tog, K1, yfwd, K2tog, P29 (30: 31: 32: 33), wrap next st and turn.

Row 5: As row 3.

Row 6: Using yarn DOUBLE, P3, K2, let second ball of yarn drop and cont as folls: yfwd, K2tog, K1, yfwd, K2tog, P to last 7 sts, K2, yfwd, K2tog, K1, yfwd, K2tog.

Row 7: (K1, yfwd, K2tog) twice, K to last 9 sts, yfwd, K2tog, K1, yfwd, using yarn DOUBLE, K2tog, K4.

Rep rows 6 and 7, 6 (6: 6: 7: 7) times more.

Shape first dart

Row 1 (WS): Using yarn DOUBLE, P3, K2, let second ball of yarn drop and cont as folls: yfwd, K2tog, K1, yfwd, K2tog, P29 (30: 31: 32: 33), wrap next st and turn.

Row 2: K to last 9 sts, yfwd, K2tog, K1, yfwd, using yarn DOUBLE, K2tog, K4.

Row 3: Using yarn DOUBLE, P3, K2, let second ball of yarn drop and cont as folls: yfwd, K2tog, K1, yfwd, K2tog, P25 (26: 27: 28: 29), wrap next st and turn.

Row 4: As row 2.

Row 5: Using yarn DOUBLE, P3, K2, let second ball of yarn drop and cont as folls: yfwd, K2tog, K1, yfwd, K2tog, P21 (22: 23: 24: 25), wrap next st and turn.

Row 6: As row 2.

Row 7: Using yarn DOUBLE, P3, K2, let second ball of yarn drop and cont as folls: yfwd, K2tog, K1, yfwd, K2tog, P to last 7 sts, K2, yfwd, K2tog, K1, yfwd, K2tog.

Row 8: (K1, yfwd, K2tog) twice, K to last 9 sts, yfwd, K2tog, K1, yfwd, using yarn DOUBLE, K2tog, K4.

Rep rows 7 and 8, 11 (13: 15: 15: 17) times more.

Shape second dart

Row 1 (WS): Using yarn DOUBLE, P3, K2, let second ball of yarn drop and cont as folls: yfwd, K2tog, K1, yfwd, K2tog, P21 (22: 23: 24: 25), wrap next st and turn.

Row 2: K to last 9 sts, yfwd, K2tog, K1, yfwd, using yarn DOUBLE, K2tog, K4.

Row 3: Using yarn DOUBLE, P3, K2, let second ball of yarn drop and cont as folls: yfwd, K2tog, K1, yfwd, K2tog, P25 (26: 27: 28: 29), wrap next st and turn.

Row 4: As row 2.

Row 5: Using yarn DOUBLE, P3, K2, let second ball of yarn drop and cont as folls: yfwd, K2tog, K1, yfwd, K2tog, P29 (30: 31: 32: 33), wrap next st and turn.

Row 6: As row 2.

Row 7: Using yarn DOUBLE, P3, K2, let second ball of yarn drop and cont as folls: yfwd, K2tog, K1, yfwd, K2tog, P to last 7 sts, K2, yfwd, K2tog, K1, yfwd, K2tog.

Row 8: (K1, yfwd, K2tog) twice, K to last 9 sts, yfwd, K2tog, K1, yfwd, using yarn DOUBLE, K2tog, K4.

Rep rows 7 and 8, 6 (6: 6: 7: 7) times more.

Next row (WS): Using yarn DOUBLE, P3, K2, let second ball of yarn drop and cont as folls: yfwd, K2tog, K1, yfwd, K2tog, P29 (30: 31: 32: 33), wrap next st and turn.

Next row: K to last 9 sts, yfwd, K2tog, K1, yfwd, using yarn DOUBLE, K2tog, K4.

Next row: Using yarn DOUBLE, P3, K2, let second ball of yarn drop and cont as folls: yfwd, K2tog, K1, yfwd, K2tog, P21 (22: 23: 24: 25), wrap next st and turn.

Next row: K to last 9 sts, yfwd, K2tog, K1, yfwd, using yarn DOUBLE, K2tog, K4.

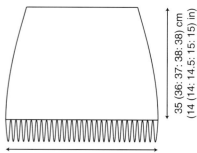

35 (36: 37: 38: 38) cm
(14: 14: 14.5: 15: 15) in

46.5 (49: 51.5: 54: 56.5) cm
(18.5 (19.5: 20.5: 21.5: 22) in)

Next row: Using yarn DOUBLE, P3, K2, let second ball of yarn drop and cont as folls: yfwd, K2tog, K1, yfwd, K2tog, P to last 7 sts, K2, yfwd, K2tog, K1, yfwd, K2tog.

Next row (RS): Cast off until 3 sts rem on left needle, fasten off st on right needle, let rem 3 sts fall from left needle and unravel down to cast-on edge to form fringe.

MAKING UP

PRESS as described on the information page.
Join side seams using back stitch, or mattress stitch if preferred.
For waist tie, make 150 cm long twisted cord and knot ends. Thread in and out of second band of eyelets near upper (shorter) row end edges.

ANNA

KIM HARGREAVES

YARN

	XS	S	M	L	XL	
To fit bust	81	86	91	97	102	cm
	32	34	36	38	40	in

Rowan Linen Print

	10	10	11	12	12	x 50gm

(photographed in Peachy 345)

NEEDLES

1 pair 7mm (no 2) (US 10½) needles
1 pair 8mm (no 0) (US 11) needles

TENSION

13 sts and 16 rows to 10 cm measured over stocking stitch using 8mm (US 11) needles.

Pattern note: Due to the heavy nature of this yarn, it has a tendency to drop in length in wear. It is therefore advisable to measure knitted sections hanging from needles, rather than laid flat.

BACK and FRONT (both alike)

Cast on 54 (58: 62: 66: 70) sts using 7mm (US 10½) needles.
Row 1 (RS): K2, ★P2, K2, rep from ★ to end.

Row 2: P2, ★K2, P2, rep from ★ to end.
These 2 rows form rib.
Work in rib for a further 4 rows, ending with a WS row.
Change to 8mm (US 11) needles.
Beg with a K row, cont in st st as folls:
Work 2 rows.
Place markers on 16th (17th: 18th: 19th: 20th) st in from both ends of last row.
Next row (dec) (RS): K to within 1 st of first marked st, K2tog (marked st is second of these 2 sts), K to second marked st, K2tog tbl (marked st is first st of these 2 sts), K to end.
Work 1 row.
Rep last 2 rows 4 times more. 44 (48: 52: 56: 60) sts.
Work 4 rows, ending with a WS row.
Next row (inc) (RS): K to first marked st, K marked st, M1, K to next marked st, M1, K marked st, K to end.
Work 3 rows.
Rep last 4 rows 4 times more. 54 (58: 62: 66: 70) sts.
Cont straight until work measures 28 cm, ending with a WS row.

Shape raglan armholes
Cast off 3 sts at beg of next 2 rows.
48 (52: 56: 60: 64) sts.

XS size only
Next row (RS): P2, K2tog, K to last 4 sts, K2tog tbl, P2.
Next row: K2, P to last 2 sts, K2.
Next row: P2, K to last 2 sts, P2.
Next row: K2, P to last 2 sts, K2.
Rep last 4 rows once more. 44 sts.

M, L and XL sizes only
Next row (RS): P2, K2tog, K to last 4 sts, K2tog tbl, P2.
Next row: K2, P2tog tbl, P to last 4 sts, P2tog, K2.
Rep last 2 rows - (-: 0: 1: 2) times more.
- (-: 52: 52: 52) sts.

All sizes
Next row (RS): P2, K2tog, K to last 4 sts, K2tog tbl, P2.
Next row: K2, P to last 2 sts, K2.
Rep last 2 rows 9 (13: 13: 12: 12) times more.
Leave rem 24 (24: 24: 26: 26) sts on a holder.

SLEEVES (both alike)

Cast on 32 (32: 34: 36: 36) sts using 7mm (US 10½) needles.

Row 1 (RS): P1 (1: 0: 1: 1), K2, ★P2, K2, rep from ★ to last 1 (1: 0: 1: 1) st, P1 (1: 0: 1: 1).
Row 2: K1 (1: 0: 1: 1), P2, ★K2, P2, rep from ★ to last 1 (1: 0: 1: 1) st, K1 (1: 0: 1: 1).
These 2 rows form rib.
Work in rib for a further 24 rows, inc 1 st at each end of 19th of these rows and ending with a WS row. 34 (34: 36: 38: 38) sts.
Change to 8mm (US 11) needles.
Beg with a K row, cont in st st as folls:
Work 2 (2: 4: 6: 4) rows.
Next row (RS): K2, M1, K to last 2 sts, M1, K2.
Working all increases as set by last row, inc 1 st at each end of every foll 8th (8th: 10th: 12th: 10th) row to 44 (44: 40: 42: 42) sts, then on every foll – (–: 8th: 10th: 8th) row until there are – (–: 46: 46: 48) sts.
Cont straight until sleeve measures 44 (44: 45: 45: 45) cm, ending with a WS row.
Shape raglan
Cast off 3 sts at beg of next 2 rows.
38 (38: 40: 40: 42) sts.
Next row (RS): P2, K2tog, K to last 4 sts, K2tog tbl, P2.
Next row: K2, P to last 2 sts, K2.
Rep last 2 rows 13 (13: 14: 14: 15) times more.
Leave rem 10 sts on a holder.
For second (left) sleeve, do not break yarn as this ball of yarn will be used to cast-off.

MAKING UP

PRESS as described on the information page.
Join both front and right back raglan seams using back stitch, or mattress stitch if preferred.
Neck edging
With RS facing and using 7mm (US 10½) needles, cast off sts of left sleeve, then front, then right sleeve, then back.
See information page for finishing instructions.

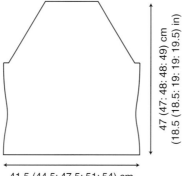

47 (47: 48: 48: 49) cm
(18.5 (18.5: 19: 19: 19.5) in)

41.5 (44.5: 47.5: 51: 54) cm
(16.5 (17.5: 18.5: 20: 21.5) in)

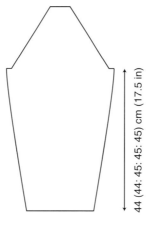

44 (44: 45: 45: 45) cm (17.5 in)

DEE

KIM HARGREAVES

YARN

	XS	S	M	L	XL	
To fit bust	81	86	91	97	102	cm
	32	34	36	38	40	in

Rowan Linen Print

| | 13 | 13 | 14 | 15 | 16 | x 50gm |

(photographed in Refresher 344)

NEEDLES

1 pair 7mm (no 2) (US 10½) needles
1 pair 8mm (no 0) (US 11) needles

TENSION

13 sts and 16 rows to 10 cm measured over stocking stitch using 8mm (US 11) needles.

Pattern note: Due to the heavy nature of this yarn, it has a tendency to drop in length in wear. It is therefore advisable to measure knitted sections hanging from needles, rather than laid flat.

BACK

Cast on 55 (59: 63: 67: 71) sts using 7mm (US 10½) needles.
Row 1 (RS): K1, ★P1, K1, rep from ★ to end.
Row 2: P1, ★K1, P1, rep from ★ to end.

These 2 rows form rib.

Work in rib for a further 6 rows, ending with a WS row.

Change to 8mm (US 11) needles.

Beg with a K row, work in st st for 8 rows.

Counting in from both ends of last row, place markers on 15th (16th: 17th: 18th: 19th) sts in from ends of row.

Row 9 (dec) (RS): K3, K2tog, K to within 1 st of first marker, sl 1, K1, psso, slip st on right needle back onto left needle, lift second st on left needle over first st and off needle, then slip same st back onto right needle (2 sts decreased - marked st is centre st), K to within 1 st of next marker, sl 1, K2tog (first of these sts is the marked st), psso, K to last 5 sts, K2tog tbl, K3. Work 9 rows.

Row 19: As row 9. 43 (47: 51: 55: 59) sts.
Work 11 rows.

Row 31: K3, M1, (K to marked st, M1, K marked st, M1) twice, K to last 3 sts, M1, K3. Work 13 rows.

Row 45: As row 31. 55 (59: 63: 67: 71) sts.
Cont straight until back measures 40 (41: 41: 42: 42) cm, ending with a WS row.

Shape armholes

Cast off 2 (3: 3: 4: 4) sts at beg of next 2 rows. 51 (53: 57: 59: 63) sts.

Dec 1 st at each end of next 3 (3: 5: 5: 7) rows, then on foll 2 alt rows.
41 (43: 43: 45: 45) sts.

Cont straight until armhole measures 20 (20: 21: 21: 22) cm, ending with a WS row.

Shape shoulders and back neck

Cast off 4 sts at beg of next 2 rows. 33 (35: 35: 37: 37) sts.

Next row (RS): Cast off 4 sts, K until there are 8 sts on right needle and turn, leaving rem sts on a holder.

Work each side of neck separately.

Cast off 4 sts at beg of next row.

Cast off rem 4 sts.

With RS facing, rejoin yarn to rem sts, cast off centre 9 (11: 11: 13: 13) sts, K to end.

Complete to match first side, reversing shapings.

FRONT

Work as given for back until 8 (8: 8: 10: 10) rows less have been worked to start of shoulder shaping, ending with a WS row.

Shape neck

Next row (RS): K17 (17: 17: 18: 18) and turn, leaving rem sts on a holder.

Work each side of neck separately.

Dec 1 st at neck edge of next 4 rows, then on foll 1 (1: 1: 2: 2) alt rows. 12 sts.

Work 1 row, ending with a WS row.

Shape shoulder

Cast off 4 sts at beg of next and foll alt row.

Work 1 row. Cast off rem 4 sts.

With RS facing, rejoin yarn to rem sts, cast off centre 7 (9: 9: 9: 9) sts, K to end.

Complete to match first side, reversing shapings.

SLEEVES (both alike)

Cast on 64 (64: 67: 70: 70) sts using 7mm (US 10½) needles.

Row 1 (RS): K1, ★P2, K1, rep from ★ to end.
Row 2: P1, ★K2, P1, rep from ★ to end.
These 2 rows form rib.

Work in rib for a further 9 rows, ending with a RS row.

Row 12 (WS): P1, ★K1, let next st drop from left needle and unravel down to cast-on edge, P1, rep from ★ to end. 43 (43: 45: 47: 47) sts.

Row 13: P2tog, ★K1, P1, rep from ★ to last 3 sts, K1, P2tog. 41 (41: 43: 45: 45) sts.

Row 14: K1, ★P1, K1, rep from ★ to end.
Row 15: P1, ★K1, P1, rep from ★ to end.
Row 16: As row 14.

Change to 8mm (US 11) needles.

Row 17 (RS): K3, K2tog, K to last 5 sts, K2tog tbl, K3.

Beg with a P row, work in st st for 3 rows.

Row 21: As row 17. 37 (37: 39: 41: 41) sts.

Beg with a P row, work in st st for 13 rows, ending with a WS row.

Next row (RS): K3, M1, K to last 3 sts, M1, K3.

Working all increases as set by last row, inc 1 st at each end of 26th (14th: 14th: 14th: 8th) and every foll 0 (12th: 14th: 14th: 10th) row until there are 41 (43: 45: 47: 49) sts.

Cont straight until sleeve measures 43 (43: 44: 44: 44) cm, ending with a WS row.

Shape top

Cast off 2 (3: 3: 4: 4) sts at beg of next 2 rows. 37 (37: 39: 39: 41) sts.

Dec 1 st at each end of next 3 rows, then on foll alt row, then on every foll 4th row until 25 (25: 27: 27: 29) sts rem.

Work 1 row, ending with a WS row.

Dec 1 st at each end of next and every foll alt row to 21 sts, then on foll 3 rows, ending with a WS row.

Cast off rem 15 sts.

MAKING UP

PRESS as described on the information page. Join right shoulder seam using back stitch, or mattress stitch if preferred.

Neckband

With RS facing and using 7mm (US 10½) needles, pick up and knit 13 (13: 13: 15: 15) sts down left side of neck, 7 (9: 9: 9: 9) sts from front, 13 (13: 13: 15: 15) sts up right side of neck, then 18 (20: 20: 22: 22) sts from back. 51 (55: 55: 61: 61) sts.

Work in rib as given for back for 10 cm.

Cast off in rib

See information page for finishing instructions, setting in sleeves using the set-in method.

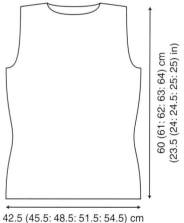

60 (61: 62: 63: 64) cm
(23.5 (24: 24.5: 25: 25) in)

42.5 (45.5: 48.5: 51.5: 54.5) cm
(16.5 (18: 19: 20.5: 21.5) in)

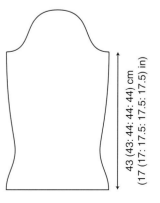

43 (43: 44: 44: 44) cm
(17 (17: 17.5: 17.5: 17.5) in)

PATRICE

KIM HARGREAVES

	XS	S	M	L	XL	
To fit bust	81	86	91	97	102	cm
	32	34	36	38	40	in

Rowan Linen Print

| A Moody | 348 | 9 | 9 | 10 | 10 | 11 | x 50gm |
| B Pip | 346 | 6 | 6 | 6 | 7 | 7 | x 50gm |

NEEDLES
1 pair 7mm (no 2) (US 10½) needles
1 pair 8mm (no 0) (US 11) needles

TENSION
13 sts and 16 rows to 10 cm measured over
stocking stitch using 8mm (US 11) needles.

Pattern note: Due to the heavy nature of this
yarn, it has a tendency to drop in length in wear.
It is therefore advisable to measure knitted
sections hanging from needles, rather than laid
flat.

LOWER BACK and FRONT (both alike)
Cast on 61 (65: 69: 73: 77) sts using 7mm
(US 10½) needles and yarn A.
Row 1 (RS): Purl.

Row 2: Purl.
Rep last 2 rows 3 times more.
Change to 8mm (US 11) needles.
Beg with a K row, cont in st st until work
measures 47 (48: 48: 49: 49) cm, ending with a
WS row. Cast off.

LEFT SLEEVE AND YOKE
Cast on 39 (39: 39: 41: 41) sts using 7mm
(US 10½) needles and yarn A.
Row 1 (RS): Purl.
Row 2: Purl.
Rep last 2 rows 3 times more.
Change to 8mm (US 11) needles and cont in
patt as folls:
Row 1 (RS): Using yarn A, knit.
Row 2: Using yarn A, purl.
Join in yarn B.
Row 3: Using yarn B, inc in first st, K to last st,
inc in last st. 41 (41: 41: 43: 43) sts.
Row 4: Using yarn B, knit.
These 4 rows form patt and start sleeve shaping.
Cont in patt, shaping sides by inc 1 st at each
end of 5th and every foll 6th row to 53 (53: 51:
57: 53) sts, then on every foll 4th row until there
are 61 (61: 63: 63: 65) sts.
Cont straight until work measures 44 (44: 45:
45: 45) cm, ending with a WS row.
Place markers at both ends of last row to denote
underarm point.

Cont straight until work measures 12.5 (14:
15.5: 17: 18.5) cm from markers, ending with a
WS row.★★
Divide for neck
Next row (RS): K29 (29: 30: 30: 31), K2tog
and turn, leaving rem sts on a holder.
30 (30: 31: 31: 32) sts.
Work each side of neck separately.
Dec 1 st at neck edge of next 2 rows, then on
foll 4th row. 27 (27: 28: 28: 29) sts.
Cont straight until work measures 23.5 (25:
26.5: 28: 29.5) cm from markers, ending with a
WS row. Cast off.
With RS facing, rejoin yarn to rem sts, K2tog,
K to end. 29 (29: 30: 30: 31) sts.
Dec 1 st at neck edge of next 3 rows.
26 (26: 27: 27: 28) sts.
Cont straight until this front yoke section
matches back yoke section to cast-off edge,
ending with a WS row. Cast off.

RIGHT SLEEVE AND YOKE
Work as given for left sleeve and yoke to ★★.
Divide for neck
Next row (RS): K28 (28: 29: 29: 30), K2tog
and turn, leaving rem sts on a holder.
29 (29: 30: 30: 31) sts.
Work each side of neck separately.
Dec 1 st at neck edge of next 3 rows.
26 (26: 27: 27: 28) sts.

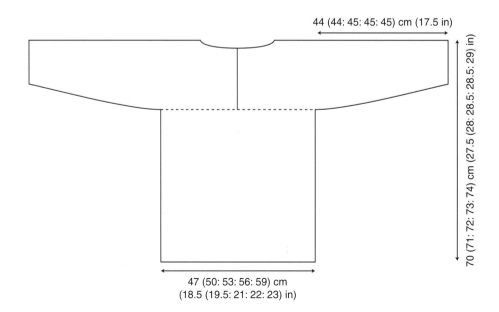

44 (44: 45: 45: 45) cm (17.5 in)

70 (71: 72: 73: 74) cm (27.5 (28: 28.5: 28.5: 29) in)

47 (50: 53: 56: 59) cm
(18.5 (19.5: 21: 22: 23) in)

Cont straight until work measures 23.5 (25: 26.5: 28: 29.5) cm from markers, ending with a WS row. Cast off.

With RS facing, rejoin yarn to rem sts, K2tog, K to end. 30 (30: 31: 31: 32) sts.

Dec 1 st at neck edge of next 2 rows, then on foll 4th row.

27 (27: 28: 28: 29) sts.

Cont straight until this back yoke section matches front yoke section to cast-off edge, ending with a WS row.

Cast off.

MAKING UP

PRESS as described on the information page. Join centre back yoke seam using back stitch, or mattress stitch if preferred.

Neckband

With RS facing, using 7mm (US 10½) needles and yarn A, starting and ending at front yoke section cast-off edges, pick up and knit 18 sts up right side of neck, 36 sts from back, then 18 sts down left side of neck. 72 sts.

Cast off knitwise (on WS).

Sew lower edge of back yoke sections to upper edge of lower back, matching sleeve/yoke markers to row-end edges of lower section. In same way, sew lower edges of front yoke sections to upper edge of lower front, positioning yoke cast-off edges so they meet at centre front. Join side and sleeve seams.

DESIGN NUMBER 14

CAPRICE

KIM HARGREAVES

YARN

	XS	S	M	L	XL	
To fit bust	81	86	91	97	102	cm
	32	34	36	38	40	in

Rowan Linen Print

| | 4 | 5 | 5 | 5 | 6 | x 50gm |

(photographed in Crush 347)

NEEDLES

1 pair 8mm (no 0) (US 11) needles

TENSION

13 sts and 18 rows to 10 cm measured over lower pattern, 11 sts and 16 rows to 10 cm measured over upper pattern using 8mm (US 11) needles.

Pattern note: Due to the heavy nature of this yarn, it has a tendency to drop in length in wear. It is therefore advisable to measure knitted sections hanging from needles, rather than laid flat.

BACK

Cast on 52 (52: 56: 60: 64) sts using 8mm (US 11) needles.

Work in lower patt as folls:

Row 1 (RS): Knit.

Row 2: P2, ★yrn, P4tog, rep from ★ to last 2 sts, P2.

Row 3: K2, ★K1, (K1, P1, K1) into yrn of previous row, rep from ★ to last 2 sts, K2.

Row 4: Knit.

Row 5: As row 2.

Row 6: As row 3.

These 6 rows form lower patt.

Cont in lower patt, dec 1 st at each end of 11th and every foll 4th row until 46 (46: 50: 54: 58) sts rem. (**note**: as number of sts varies whilst working patt, do NOT count sts after patt row 2 or 5.)

Work 2 rows, end with patt row 3 and a RS row.

Next row (WS): K2 (4: 3: 2: 4), K2tog, ★K3 (4: 5: 4: 4), K2tog, rep from ★ to last 2 (4: 3: 2: 4) sts, K to end. 37 (39: 43: 45: 49) sts.

Cont in upper patt as folls:

Row 1 (RS): Purl.

Row 2: K1, ★yfwd, K2tog, rep from ★ to end.

Row 3: Purl.

Row 4: ★Sl 1, K1, psso, yfwd, rep from ★ to last st, K1.

These 4 rows form upper patt.

Cont in upper patt, shaping side seams by inc 1 st at each end of 7th and every foll 10th row until there are 41 (43: 47: 49: 53) sts, taking inc sts into patt.

Cont straight until back measures 34 (35: 35: 36: 36) cm, ending with a **RS** row.

Next row (WS): P7 (8: 8: 10: 10), patt to last 7 (8: 8: 10: 10) sts, P to end.

Shape armholes

Next row (RS): Cast off 7 (8: 8: 10: 10) sts, K until there are 2 sts on right needle, purl to last 9 (10: 10: 12: 12) sts, K to end.

Next row: Cast off 7 (8: 8: 10: 10) sts, P until there are 2 sts on right needle, patt to last 2 sts, P1, pick up loop lying between needles and place this loop on right needle (note: this loop does NOT count as a st), slip last st purlwise. 27 (27: 31: 29: 33) sts.

Next row (dec) (RS): K tog tbl first st and the loop, K3tog tbl, purl to last 4 sts, K3tog, pick up loop lying between needles and place this loop on right needle (**note**: this loop does NOT count as a st), slip last st knitwise.

Next row (dec): P tog first st and the loop, P1, patt to last 2 sts, P1, pick up loop lying between needles and place this loop on right needle, slip last st purlwise.

Last 2 rows set slip st and st st edging and decreases.

Keeping sts and decreases correct as set, cont as folls:

Dec 2 sts at each end of next and foll 1 (1: 2: 1: 2) alt rows, then 1 st at each end of every foll 4th row until 11 (11: 11: 13: 13) sts rem.
Work 7 (7: 7: 9: 9) rows, ending with a WS row.
Next row (RS): Patt 2 sts, M1, purl to last 2 sts, M1, patt to end.
Work 1 row.
Rep last 2 rows once more. 15 (15: 15: 17: 17) sts.
Next row (RS): Patt 2 sts, M1, purl to last 2 sts, M1, patt to end.
Next row: Patt 2 sts, M1P, P to last 2 sts, M1P, patt to end. 19 (19: 19: 21: 21) sts.
Shape back neck
Next row (RS): Patt 2 sts, M1, K2 and turn, leaving rem sts on a holder.
Work each side of neck separately.
Next row: P2tog, P1, M1P, patt 2 sts. 5 sts.
Next row: Patt 2 sts, M1, K1, K2tog.
Next row: P4, patt last st.
Cast off rem 5 sts.
With RS facing, rejoin yarn to rem sts, cast off centre 11 (11: 11: 13: 13) sts, K to last 2 sts, M1, patt 2 sts. 5 sts.
Complete to match first side, reversing shapings.

FRONT

Work as given for back until 4 rows less have been worked than on back to beg of armhole shaping, ending with a WS row.
Place marker on centre st of last row.
Divide for neck
Next row (RS): Purl to within 2 sts of marked st, K1, pick up loop lying between needles and place this loop on right needle, slip next st knitwise and turn, leaving rem sts on a holder. 20 (21: 23: 24: 26) sts.
Work each side of neck separately.
Next row: P tog first st and the loop, P1, patt to end.
Next row: Purl to last 4 sts, K3tog, pick up loop lying between needles and place this loop on right needle, slip last st knitwise.
Next row: P tog first st and the loop, P1, patt to last 7 (8: 8: 10: 10) sts, P to end.
Shape armhole
Next row (RS): Cast off 3 (4: 6: 5: 7) sts, K until there are 2 sts on right needle, patt to last 2 sts, K1, pick up loop lying between needles and place this loop on right needle, slip last st knitwise. 15 (15: 15: 17: 17) sts.

Next row: P tog first st and the loop, P1, patt to last 2 sts, P1, pick up loop lying between needles and place this loop on right needle, slip last st purlwise.
Next row: K tog tbl first st and the loop, K3tog tbl, patt to last 4 sts, K3tog, pick up loop lying between needles and place this loop on right needle, slip last st knitwise.
Next row: P tog first st and the loop, P1, patt to last 2 sts, P1, pick up loop lying between needles and place this loop on right needle, slip last st purlwise.
Last 2 rows set slip st and st st edging and decreases.
Keeping sts and decreases correct as set, cont as folls:
Dec 2 sts at neck edge of 5th row, then 1 (1: 1: 2: 2) sts on foll 8th row **and at same time** dec 2 sts at armhole edge of next row, then 1 (1: 1: 2: 2) sts on foll 6th row. 5 sts.
Work 15 (15: 17: 17: 19) rows, ending with a WS row. Cast off rem 5 sts.
With RS facing, rejoin yarn to rem sts, K2tog, K1, patt to end.
Complete to match first side, reversing shapings.

MAKING UP

PRESS as described on the information page.
Back neck edging
With RS facing and using 8mm (US 11) needles, pick up and knit 18 (18: 18: 20: 20) sts across back neck edge. Cast off knitwise (on WS).
Join both shoulder seams using back stitch, or mattress stitch if preferred.
See information page for finishing instructions.

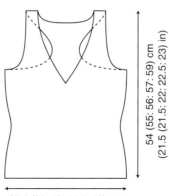

37.5 (39: 43: 44.5: 48) cm
(15 (15.5: 17: 17.5: 19) in)

54 (55: 56: 57: 59) cm
(21.5 (21.5: 22: 22.5: 23) in)

SOPHIE

KIM HARGREAVES

YARN

	XS	S	M	L	XL	
To fit bust	81	86	91	97	102	cm
	32	34	36	38	40	in

Rowan Linen Print

		XS	S	M	L	XL		
A	Peachy	345	4	4	4	5	5	x 50gm
B	Blush	342	1	1	1	1	1	x 50gm
C	Cocktail	349	1	1	1	1	1	x 50gm

NEEDLES

1 pair 7mm (no 2) (US 10½) needles
1 pair 8mm (no 0) (US 11) needles

TENSION

13 sts and 16 rows to 10 cm measured over stocking stitch using 8mm (US 11) needles.

BACK

Cast on 48 (52: 56: 60: 64) sts using 7mm (US 10½) needles and yarn A.
Row 1 (RS): Purl.
Row 2: Purl.
Change to 8mm (US 11) needles.
Place markers on 13th (14th: 15th: 16th: 17th) st in from both ends of row, and place marker between centre 2 sts.

Cont in patt as folls:

Row 1 (RS): K1, K2tog, K to first marked st, M1, K marked st, M1, K to within 2 sts of second marker, K2tog tbl, slip marker to right needle, K2tog, K to next marked st, M1, K marked st, M1, K to last 3 sts, K2tog tbl, K1.

Row 2: Purl.

These 2 rows form patt.

Keeping patt correct, cont as folls:

Join in yarn B.

Using yarn B, work 2 rows.

Using yarn A, work 2 rows.

Join in yarn C.

Using yarn C, work 2 rows.

Using yarn B, work 1 row.

Next row (dec) (WS): Using yarn B, P2, P2tog tbl, P to last 4 sts, P2tog, P2.

46 (50: 54: 58: 62) sts.

Working all decreases as set by last row, and noting that **ALL** shaping will be worked on **WS** rows, cont as folls:

Using yarn C, work 2 rows.

Using yarn A, work 2 rows, dec 1 st at each end of second of these rows.

44 (48: 52: 56: 60) sts.

Using yarn B, work 2 rows.

Break off yarn B and yarn C and cont using yarn A **only**.

Dec 1 st at each end of 2nd row.

42 (46: 50: 54: 58) sts.

Work 7 (9: 9: 11: 11) rows, ending with a RS row.

Next row (inc) (WS): P2, M1, P to last 2 sts, M1, P2.★★

Working all increases as set by last row, inc 1 st at each end of every foll 8th row until there are 48 (52: 56: 60: 64) sts.

Divide for neck

Next row (RS): Patt to within 3 sts of second marker, K2tog tbl, pick up loop lying between needles and place this loop on right needle (**note**: this loop does NOT count as a st), slip next st knitwise and turn, leaving rem sts on a holder.

24 (26: 28: 30: 32) sts.

Work each side of neck separately.

★★★**Next row (dec) (WS):** P tog first st and the loop (to form slip st edging), P2tog tbl (to dec 1 st), patt to end.

23 (25: 27: 29: 31) sts.

Last 2 rows set slip st edging and back neck decreases.

Keeping sts correct as now set, dec 1 st at neck edge of 2nd and foll 2 alt rows.

20 (22: 24: 26: 28) sts.

Shape armhole

Next row (RS): Cast off 4 (5: 6: 5: 6) sts (one st on right needle), K2tog (to match inc before next marked st), patt to end.

16 (17: 18: 21: 22) sts.

Next row (dec) (WS): Patt 1 st, P2tog tbl, P to last st, pick up loop lying between needles and place this loop on right needle (**note**: this loop does NOT count as a st), slip last st purlwise. 15 (16: 17: 20: 21) sts.

Next row (RS): K tog tbl first st and the loop, patt to end.

Last 2 rows set slip st edging along armhole edge.

Keeping slip st edging correct at both ends of rows, cont as folls:

Next row (WS): Patt 1 st, P2tog tbl, P to last 4 sts, P3tog, patt 1 st.

12 (13: 14: 17: 18) sts.

Working all armhole decreases as set by last row, dec 1 st at neck edge of 4th (2nd: 2nd: 2nd: 2nd) and foll 0 (0: 1: 2: 3) alt rows, then 1 (2: 2: 2: 2) foll 4th rows **and at same time** dec 2 sts at armhole edge of 4th and foll – (–: –: 4th: 4th) row, then 1st on foll 4th row.

7 sts.

Cont straight until armhole measures 19 (19: 20: 20: 21) cm, ending with a WS row.

Shape shoulder

Cast off rem 7 sts.

With RS facing, rejoin yarn to rem sts and cont as folls:

Next row (RS): K1, K2tog (to match inc before next marked st), patt to end.

24 (26: 28: 30: 32) sts.

Next row: P to last 3 sts, P2tog (to dec 1 st), pick up loop lying between needles and place this loop on right needle, slip last st purlwise.

23 (25: 27: 29: 31) sts.

Last 2 rows set slip st edging and front slope decreases.

Keeping sts correct as now set, dec 1 st at neck edge of 2nd and foll 2 alt rows.

20 (22: 24: 26: 28) sts.

Work 1 row, ending with a RS row.

Shape armhole

Cast off 4 (5: 6: 5: 6) sts at beg and dec 1 st at end (neck edge) of next row.

15 (16: 17: 20: 21) sts.

Now working slip st edging at both ends of rows, cont as folls:

Work 1 row.

Next row (WS): Patt 1 st, P3tog tbl, P to last 3 sts, P2tog, patt 1 st. 12 (13: 14: 17: 18) sts.

Working all armhole decreases as set by last row, dec 1 st at neck edge of 4th (2nd: 2nd: 2nd: 2nd) and foll 0 (0: 1: 2: 3) alt rows, then 1 (2: 2: 2: 2) foll 4th rows **and at same time** dec 2 sts at armhole edge of 4th and foll – (–: –: 4th: 4th) row, then 1st on foll 4th row. 7 sts.

Cont straight until armhole measures 19 (19: 20: 20: 21) cm, ending with a WS row.

Shape shoulder

Cast off rem 7 sts.

FRONT

Work as given for back to ★★.

Working all increases as set by last row, cont as folls:

Work 4 rows, ending with a WS row.

Divide for front opening

Next row (RS): Patt 22 (24: 26: 28: 30) sts and turn, leaving rem sts on a holder.

Work each side of neck separately.

Work 11 rows, inc 1 st at side seam edge of 3rd and foll 8th of these rows and ending with a WS row. 24 (26: 28: 30: 32) sts.

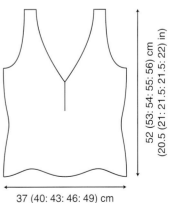

52 (53: 54: 55: 56) cm
(20.5 (21: 21.5: 21.5: 22) in)

37 (40: 43: 46: 49) cm
(14.5 (15.5: 17: 18: 19.5) in)

Shape neck

Next row (RS): Patt to last 3 sts, K2tog tbl (to match in after last marker), pick up loop lying between needles and place this loop on right needle, slip last st knitwise.

24 (26: 28: 30: 32) sts.

Complete this side of neck as given for back from ★★★.

With RS facing, rejoin yarn to rem sts, patt to end.

Complete second side to match first, reversing shapings.

MAKING UP

PRESS as described on the information page.

Join both shoulder seams using back stitch, or mattress stitch if preferred.

See information page for finishing instructions.

Catch stitch front opening edges together at beg of front neck shaping.

INES

KIM HARGREAVES

YARN

	XS	S	M	L	XL
To fit bust	81	86	91	97	102 cm
	32	34	36	38	40 in

Rowan Linen Print

A Blush	342	9	10	10	11	12	x 50gm
B Peachy	345	1	1	1	1	1	x 50gm
C Refresher	344	1	1	1	1	1	x 50gm

NEEDLES

1 pair 7mm (no 2) (US 10½) needles
1 pair 8mm (no 0) (US 11) needles

TENSION

13 sts and 16 rows to 10 cm measured over stocking stitch using 8mm (US 11) needles.

Pattern note: Due to the heavy nature of this yarn, it has a tendency to drop in length in wear. It is therefore advisable to measure knitted sections hanging from needles, rather than laid flat.

BACK

Cast on 54 (58: 62: 66: 70) sts using 7mm (US 10½) needles and yarn A.

Row 1 (RS): Purl.
Row 2: Purl.

Change to 8mm (US 11) needles and cont in patt as folls:

Row 1 (RS): K5 (2: 4: 0: 2), (yfwd, K3, K2tog tbl) 0 (1: 1: 0: 0) times, ★K2tog, K3, yfwd, K1, yfwd, K3, K2tog tbl, rep from ★ to last 5 (7: 9: 0: 2) sts, (K2tog, K3, yfwd) 0 (1: 1: 0: 0) times, K5 (2: 4: 0: 2).

Row 2: Purl.

These 2 rows form patt.

Keeping patt correct, cont as folls:

Work 4 rows.

Join in yarn B.

Using yarn B, work 2 rows, dec 1 st at each end of first of these rows. 52 (56: 60: 64: 68) sts.

Join in yarn C.

Using yarn C, work 2 rows.

Using yarn A, work 2 rows, dec 1 st at each end of first of these rows. 50 (54: 58: 62: 66) sts.

Using yarn C, work 2 rows.

Using yarn B, work 2 rows, dec 1 st at each end of first of these rows. 48 (52: 56: 60: 64) sts.

Break off yarn B and yarn C and cont using yarn A **only**.

Dec 1 st at each end of 3rd row.

46 (50: 54: 58: 62) sts.

Work 5 rows, ending with a WS row.

Inc 1 st at each end of next and every foll 6th row until there are 54 (58: 62: 66: 70) sts, taking inc sts into st st until there are sufficient to work in patt.

Cont straight until back measures 32 (33: 33: 34: 34) cm, ending with a WS row.

Shape armholes

Keeping patt correct, cast off 2 (3: 3: 4: 4) sts at beg of next 2 rows. 50 (52: 56: 58: 62) sts.

Dec 1 st at each end of next 3 (3: 5: 5: 7) rows, then on foll 0 (1: 0: 1: 0) alt row.

44 (44: 46: 46: 48) sts.

Cont straight until armhole measures 20 (20: 21: 21: 22) cm, ending with a WS row.

Shape shoulders and back neck

Cast off 4 sts at beg of next 2 rows.

36 (36: 38: 38: 40) sts.

Next row (RS): Cast off 4 sts, patt until there are 8 (7: 8: 7: 8) sts on right needle and turn, leaving rem sts on a holder.

Work each side of neck separately.

Cast off 4 sts at beg of next row.

Cast off rem 4 (3: 4: 3: 4) sts.
With RS facing, rejoin yarn to rem sts, cast off centre 12 (14: 14: 16: 16) sts, patt to end.
Complete to match first side, reversing shapings.

FRONT

Work as given for back until 10 (10: 10: 12: 12) rows less have been worked to start of shoulder shaping, ending with a WS row.

Shape neck

Next row (RS): Patt 18 (17: 18: 18: 19) sts and turn, leaving rem sts on a holder.
Work each side of neck separately.
Dec 1 st at neck edge of next 4 rows, then on foll 2 (2: 2: 3: 3) alt rows. 12 (11: 12: 11: 12) sts.
Work 1 row, ending with a WS row.

Shape shoulder

Cast off 4 sts at beg of next and foll alt row.
Work 1 row.
Cast off rem 4 (3: 4: 3: 4) sts.
With RS facing, rejoin yarn to rem sts, cast off centre 8 (10: 10: 10: 10) sts, patt to end.
Complete to match first side, reversing shapings.

SLEEVES (both alike)

Cast on 34 (34: 36: 38: 38) sts using 7mm (US 10½) needles and yarn A.
Row 1 (RS): Purl.
Row 2: Purl.
Change to 8mm (US 11) needles and cont in patt as folls:
Row 1 (RS): K1 (1: 2: 3: 3), *yfwd, K3, K2tog tbl, K2tog, K3, yfwd, K1, rep from * to last 0 (0: 1: 2: 2) sts, K0 (0: 1: 2: 2).
Row 2: Purl.
These 2 rows form patt.
Keeping patt correct, cont as folls:
Work 4 rows.

Join in yarn B.
Using yarn B, work 2 rows.
Join in yarn C.
Using yarn C, work 2 rows.
Using yarn A, work 2 rows.
Using yarn C, work 2 rows.
Using yarn B, work 2 rows.
Break off yarn B and yarn C and cont using yarn A **only**.
Cont in patt, shaping sides by inc 1 st at each end of next and every foll 16th (12th: 16th: 16th: 16th) row to 38 (40: 42: 44: 44) sts, then on every foll 14th (10th: 14th: 14th: 14th) row until there are 42 (44: 44: 46: 46) sts.
Cont straight until sleeve measures 43 (43: 44: 44: 44) cm, ending with a WS row.

Shape top

Keeping patt correct, cast off 2 (3: 3: 4: 4) sts at beg of next 2 rows. 38 sts.
Dec 1 st at each end of next 3 rows, then on foll alt row, then on every foll 4th row until 26 sts rem.
Work 1 row, ending with a WS row.
Dec 1 st at each end of next and foll alt row, then on foll 3 rows, ending with a WS row.
Cast off rem 16 sts.

MAKING UP

PRESS as described on the information page.
Join right shoulder seam using back stitch, or mattress stitch if preferred.

Neckband

With RS facing, using 7mm (US 10½) needles and yarn A, pick up and knit 12 (12: 12: 14: 14) sts down left side of neck, 8 (10: 10: 10: 10) sts from front, 12 (12: 12: 14: 14) sts up right side of neck, then 20 (22: 22: 24: 24) sts from back. 52 (56: 56: 62: 62) sts.
Cast off knitwise (on WS).
See information page for finishing instructions, setting in sleeves using the set-in method.

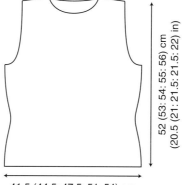

41.5 (44.5: 47.5: 51: 54) cm
(16.5 (17.5: 18.5: 20: 21.5) in)

52 (53: 54: 55: 56) cm
(20.5 (21: 21.5: 21.5: 22) in)

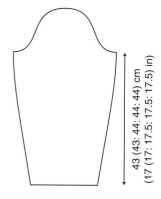

43 (43: 44: 44: 44) cm
(17 (17: 17.5: 17.5: 17.5) in)

BIANCA

KIM HARGREAVES

YARN

	XS	S	M	L	XL	
To fit bust	81	86	91	97	102	cm
	32	34	36	38	40	in

Rowan Linen Print

| | 12 | 13 | 13 | 14 | 15 | x 50gm |

(photographed in Crush 347)

NEEDLES

1 pair 7mm (no 2) (US 10½) needles
1 pair 8mm (no 0) (US 11) needles

TENSION

10 sts and 16 rows to 10 cm measured over pattern using 8mm (US 11) needles.

Pattern note: Due to the heavy nature of this yarn, it has a tendency to drop in length in wear. It is therefore advisable to measure knitted sections hanging from needles, rather than laid flat.

BACK and FRONT (both alike)

Cast on 50 (50: 54: 58: 58) sts using 7mm (US 10½) needles.
Row 1 (RS): P2, *K2, P2, rep from * to end.
Row 2: K2, *P2, K2, rep from * to end.

These 2 rows form rib.
Work in rib for a further 16 rows, dec 1 (0: 1: 1: 0) st at each end of last row and ending with a WS row. 48 (50: 52: 56: 58) sts.
Change to 8mm (US 11) needles and cont in patt as folls:
Row 1 (RS): P1, *yrn, P2tog, rep from * to last st, P1.
Row 2: As row 1.
These 2 rows form patt.
Cont in patt until work measures 45 (46: 46: 47: 47) cm, ending with a WS row.

Shape armholes

Keeping patt correct, cast off 4 sts at beg of next 2 rows. 40 (42: 44: 48: 50) sts.
Cont straight until armhole measures 22.5 (22.5: 23.5: 23.5: 24.5) cm, ending with a WS row.

Shape neck

Next row (RS): Patt 11 (11: 12: 13: 14) sts and turn, leaving rem sts on a holder.
Work each side of neck separately.
Dec 1 st at neck edge of next 2 rows.
9 (9: 10: 11: 12) sts.
Work 1 row, ending with a WS row.

Shape shoulder

Cast off 4 (4: 4: 5: 5) sts at beg and dec 1 st at end of next row.
Work 1 row. Cast off rem 4 (4: 5: 5: 6) sts.
With RS facing, rejoin yarn to rem sts, cast off centre 18 (20: 20: 22: 22) sts, patt to end.
Complete to match first side, reversing shapings.

SLEEVES (both alike)

Cast on 26 (26: 30: 30: 30) sts using 7mm (US 10½) needles.
Work in rib as given for back and front for 20 rows, ending with a WS row.
Change to 8mm (US 11) needles and cont in patt as given for back and front, inc 1 st at each end of 3rd and every foll 4th row until there are 50 (50: 52: 52: 54) sts, taking inc sts into rev st st until there are sufficient to work in patt.
Cont straight until sleeve measures 48 (48: 49: 49: 49) cm, ending with a WS row.
Cast off loosely.

MAKING UP

PRESS as described on the information page.
Join right shoulder seam using back stitch, or mattress stitch if preferred.

Neckband

With RS facing and using 7mm (US 10½) needles, pick up and knit 6 sts down left side of front neck, 17 (19: 19: 21: 21) sts from front, 6 sts up right side of front neck, 6 sts down right side of back neck, 17 (19: 19: 21: 21) sts from back, then 6 sts up left side of back neck. 58 (62: 62: 66: 66) sts.
Work in rib as given for back and front for 7.5 cm.
Cast off in rib.
See information page for finishing instructions, setting in sleeves using the square set-in method.

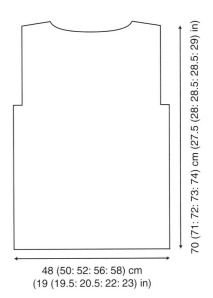

48 (50: 52: 56: 58) cm
(19 (19.5: 20.5: 22: 23) in)

70 (71: 72: 73: 74) cm (27.5 (28: 28.5: 28.5: 29) in)

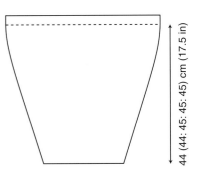

44 (44: 45: 45: 45) cm (17.5 in)

TENSION

Obtaining the correct tension is perhaps the single factor which can make the difference between a successful garment and a disastrous one. It controls both the shape and size of an article, so **any** variation, can distort the finished look of the garment. We recommend that you knit a square in pattern and/or stocking stitch of perhaps 5 more stitches and rows than those given in the tension note. Press the finished square under a damp cloth and mark out the central 10cm square. If you have too many stitches to 10cm try again using thicker needles, if you have too few stitches to 10cm try again using finer needles.

SIZING AND SIZE DIAGRAM NOTE

The instructions are given for the smallest size. Where they vary, work the figures in brackets for the larger sizes. **One set of figures refers to all sizes**. Included with every pattern in this magazine is a '**size diagram**', the purpose of which is to enable you to accurately achieve a perfect fitting garment without the need for worry during knitting. The size diagram shows the finished width of the garment at the under-arm point, and it is this measurement that the knitter should choose first. Next look at the corresponding length for that size; if you are not happy with the total length which we recommend, adjust your own garment before beginning your armhole shaping - any adjustment after this point will mean that your sleeve will not fit into your garment easily - don't forget to take your adjustment into account if there is any side seam shaping. Finally, look at the sleeve length; the size diagram shows the finished sleeve measurement, taking into account any top-arm insertion length. Measure your body between the centre of your neck and your wrist, this measurement should correspond to half the garment width plus the sleeve length. Again, your sleeve length may be adjusted, but remember to take into consideration your sleeve increases if you do adjust the length - you must increase more frequently than the pattern states to shorten your sleeve, less frequently to lengthen it.

FINISHING INSTRUCTIONS

After working for hours knitting a garment, it seems a great pity that many garments are spoiled because such little care is taken in the pressing and finishing process.

PRESSING

Darn in all ends neatly along the selvage edge or a colour join, as appropriate. Block out each piece of knitting using pins and gently press each piece, omitting the ribs, using a warm iron over a damp cloth. **Tip**: Take special care to press the edges, as this will make sewing up both easier and neater.

STITCHING

When stitching the pieces together, remember to match areas of colour and texture very carefully where they meet.
Use a seam stitch such as back stitch or mattress stitch for all main knitting seams, and join all ribs and neckband with a flat seam unless otherwise stated.

CONSTRUCTION

Having completed the pattern instructions, join left shoulder and neckband seams as detailed above. Sew the top of the sleeve to the body of the garment using the method detailed in the pattern, referring to the appropriate guide:

Square set-in sleeves: Set sleeve head into armhole, the straight sides at top of sleeve to form a neat right-angle to cast-off sts at armhole on back and front.

Shallow set-in sleeves: Join cast-off sts at beg of armhole shaping to cast-off sts at start of sleeve-head shaping. Sew sleeve head into armhole, easing in shapings.

Set-in sleeves: Set in sleeve, easing sleeve head into armhole.

Join side and sleeve seams.
Slip stitch pocket edgings and linings into place.
Sew on buttons to correspond with buttonholes.
After sewing up, press seams and hems.
Ribbed welts and neckbands and any areas of garter stitch should not be pressed.

ABBREVIATIONS

K	knit
P	purl
st(s)	stitch(es)
inc	increas(e)(ing)
dec	decreas(e)(ing)
st st	stocking stitch (1 row K, 1 row P)
garter st	garter stitch (K every row)
beg	begin(ning)
foll	following
rem	remain(ing)
rev	revers(e)(ing)
rep	repeat
alt	alternate
cont	continue
patt	pattern
tog	together
mm	millimetres
cm	centimetres
in(s)	inch(es)
RS	right side
WS	wrong side
sl 1	slip one stitch
psso	pass slipped stitch over
p2sso	pass 2 slipped stitches over
tbl	through back of loop
M1	make one stitch by picking up horizontal loop before next stitch and knitting into back of it
M1P	make one stitch by picking up horizontal loop before next stitch and purling into back of it
yfwd	yarn forward
yrn	yarn round needle
yon	yarn over needle

EXPERIENCE RATINGS

= Easy, straight forward knitting

= Suitable for the average knitter

= For the more experienced knitter

STOCKIST INFORMATION

ROWAN OVERSEAS DISTRIBUTORS

AUSTRALIA
Australian Country Spinners
314 Albert Street
Brunswick
Victoria 3056
Tel: (03) 9380 3888

BELGIUM
Pavan
Meerlaanstraat 73
B9860 Balegem (Oosterzele)
Tel: (32) 9 221 8594

CANADA
Diamond Yarn
9697 St Laurent
Montreal
Quebec H3L 2N1
Tel: (514) 388 6188
www.diamondyarns.com

Diamond Yarn (Toronto)
155 Martin Ross, Unit 3
Toronto
Ontario M3J 2L9
Tel: (416) 736 6111
www.diamondyarns.com

DENMARK
Individual stockists -
please contact Rowan for details

FRANCE
Elle Tricot
8 Rue du Coq
67000 Strasbourg
Tel: (33) 3 88 23 03 13
www.elletricote.com

GERMANY
Wolle & Design
Wolfshovener Strasse 76
52428 Julich-Stetternich
Tel : (49) 2461 54735
www.wolleundesign.de

HOLLAND
de Afstap
Oude Leliestraat 12
1015 AW Amsterdam
Tel : (31) 20 6231445

HONG KONG
East Unity Co Ltd
Unit B2
7/F, Block B
Kailey Industrial Centre
12 Fung Yip Street
Chai Wan
Tel : (852) 2869 7110

ICELAND
Storkurinn
Laugavegi 59
Reykjavik
Tel: (354) 551 82 58

JAPAN
Puppy Co Ltd
TOC Building
7-22-17 Nishigotanda
Shinagwa-Ku
Tokyo
Tel : (81) 3 3494 2435

NEW ZEALAND
Individual stockists -
please contact Rowan for details

NORWAY
Pa Pinne
Tennisun 3D
0777 OSLO
Tel: (47) 909 62 818
www.paapinne.no

SWEDEN
Wincent
Norrtulsgaten 65
11345 Stockholm
Tel: (46) 8 673 70 60

U.S.A.
Rowan USA
4 Townsend West
Suite 8, Nashua
New Hampshire 03063
Tel: (1 603) 886 5041/5043

For details of U.K. stockists or any other information concerning this book please contact:

Rowan Yarns, Green Lane Mill, Holmfirth, West Yorkshire HD9 2DX
Tel: +44 (0)1484 681881   Fax: +44 (0)1484 687920
Email: linenprint@knitrowan.com www.knitrowan.com